Woman of
Karyn Solange Forbes
Substance

Woman of

Karyn Solange Forbes

Substance

Trinity Hills Publishing

Copyright © 2021 Karyn Solange Forbes

All rights reserved. No part of this publication may be reproduced, distributed, or transmitted in any form or by any means, including photocopying, recording, or other electronic or mechanical methods, without prior written permission of the publisher, except in the case of brief quotations and certain other noncommercial uses permitted by copyright law.

ISBN: 978-9-7682902-5-0

Printed in the United States of America.

Trinity Hills Publishing

www.trinityhillspublishing.com

"A great way to strive through adversities and still become successful. (I CAN DO ALL THINGS THROUGH CHRIST WHO STRENGTHENS ME)."

— Philippians 4:13

Contents

Acknowledgements	9
Introduction	11
Life Growing Up in Tobago	15
My Home Life	15
Being Part of an Extended Family	15
Village Life	17
Tobago Cuisine	20
Chapter 1 The Start of My Football Journey	23
Chapter 2 Playing Football at the Primary and Secondary School Levels	27
Chapter 3 Attending University in the United States of America	31
Chapter 4 College Culture Shock Soccer vs Football	35
Chapter 5 My Second Stop Transferring to West Texas	41
Chapter 6 Balancing Athletics and Academics	47
Chapter 7 Distractions in College	51
Chapter 8 Humorous College Moments	55
Chapter 9 National Career	61
Chapter 10 Positives About the National Team	69
Chapter 11 Airport Activities; Mentionable Memories	73

Chapter 12 Playing Professional Football in Iceland	77
Chapter 13 Iceland The Scenery, People, and Food	83
Chapter 14 Stumbling Blocks in My Career	87
Chapter 15 The Positive Impact of Football in My Life	91
Chapter 16 Fearful of Failure or Lack of Faith?	93
Chapter 17 More Women Becoming Successful in Sports and Globally	97
Chapter 18 Fellow Woman of Substance, Do Not Settle	101
Chapter 19 Personal Life	105
Chapter 20 My Driving Force	113
Chapter 21 My Second Motivator	117
Chapter 22 My Third Motivator	123
Chapter 23 Society's Ability to Affect Our Thinking and Our Lives	125
Chapter 24 Leaders Who Have Inspired Me	129
Chapter 25 Leaders - Are They Born or Made?	139
Chapter 26 Important People Met Along My Journey	145
Chapter 27 Meet April Heinrich	149
Chapter 28 Caribbean Power House Creating History	155
Chapter 29 Who is My Role Model?	157
Chapter 30 "Kick it With Karyn"	161
Chapter 31 Future Plans - I Needed to Consult With Covid	167
Chapter 32 Plans for a Family	173
Chapter 33 A Proud Moment The Grand Finale	177
About The Author	181

Acknowledgements

I would like to specifically thank GOD for the mercies, health, strength, and knowledge which He has provided along my life's journey thus far. Since I grew to love Jesus, He has been my steadfast light and shining armour, and without Him, I would not have been able to reach where I am today.

Other important people in my life to whom I would like to extend gratitude, are my mother, Sonia Forbes, my best friend's mother, Gretel Ann Goodridge Belgrave, my guardian, Burt Stewart, and his mother, for accepting me as their own. I would also like to include my father, Kelvin Sandy, who though having not always been in my life, has made some contribution to my development. I wish to thank as well, my loving sisters - Kimika and Sachelle Forbes, and Maya Friday.

It would be remiss of me if I failed to mention other important family members who have been there for me: Kimone Quashie, Resia Forbes, Wynette Forbes, Patsy Forbes, Lorraine Forbes, to name a few, have all played a significant role in my life. Kimone has filled the gap in so many ways, always wanting the best for me, and for that I cannot thank her enough.

I also have close friends that I can now call my sisters and brothers - they are Victoria Swift, Tasha St Louis, Sharice Arthur, Khadisha and Khadidra Debesette, Akilah Arthur, Tammica Hutchinson, Shanelle Arjoon, Saphia Holder John, Dixie Ann Daniel, Tkeyah Philips, Kyle Andrews, and Shane Sandy. I have one best friend - Rhea Belgrave - we have been friends for a very long time and she knows me very well.

My college coach, Chad Webb has been like a father to me. He and his wife, Joy Webb, took special care of me and I love them dearly.

Introduction

The process of naming this book took me some time, as I went back and forth brainstorming names. During the process, I decided to consult with my cousin Shane Sandy, and we both came up with the name "Woman of Substance". To my mind, the name Woman of Substance is ideal, as it is a true reflection of me, and in sync with my story. I also think the name "Woman of Substance" is a perfect example of the message I would like to convey to my readers. When I think about a "woman of substance", I envision a positive woman, a woman with purpose, a woman of power, a self-motivated woman, a goal-oriented woman, and an empowered woman, just to name a few of a long list of positive attributes.

This brings me to one of my favorite quotes from Nelson Mandela, "Our deepest fear is not that we are inadequate. Our deepest fear is that we are powerful beyond measure". This quote inspires me simply because it shows that there are no limits in life, especially when you develop the attitude of a "woman of substance", who believes that nothing but you can stop you. Once you believe in yourself, push yourself towards achieving your goals and refrain from the practice of limiting yourself, you find that you are capable of achieving anything your heart desires.

While penning this book, I was strongly inclined to believe that the content and especially its telling of my life story would have the power to change lives. If you are looking for someone's story which acts as a living testimony, to propel you towards initiating positive personal change, then your desire will surely be fulfilled as you peruse the pages of this book. The comments contained herein, on my journey to becoming a "woman of substance", the confidence I have developed, the knowledge I have gained along the way, and the way it has impacted my life positively, can act as a great motivational guide to inspire other women to harness their inner strength as they to navigate their paths to becoming women of substance.

Apart from gaining some insight into my life, as you read through the book, you will discover chapters that address the history of women's rights, and which highlight other women's journeys to becoming successful leaders, both in the personal and professional spheres of their lives. It is my hope that by highlighting how women of the past gained rights, modern women would be led to appreciate the many privileges we have today, and to which we were not privy in the past. The book seeks not to foster a competitive spirit, women against men, but rather to bring about the understanding that the only person with whom one is in competition against, is oneself, and that there is nothing wrong with taking advantage of one's opportunities to become the best version of oneself.

It is my belief that any female can be a woman of substance. It simply boils down to how badly you want it and recognising that self-growth is a personal project, which can only be initiated through a change in your mindset. Your journey to success may not directly imitate mine, but you can definitely use my story to fuel your ambition of wanting to accomplish your dreams.

One of my favorite sayings which helped me along my journey of becoming a woman of substance was, "Anything you would like to accomplish in life is on the other side of fear". Don't let fear or doubt hold you back from making that decision or taking that step that could change your life completely. Since evolving into a woman of substance, I have noticed that there is always a solution to any situation you may face. It's totally up to you to find a way. Don't sit down and make excuses, really take the opportunity to challenge yourself to find a way. Yes, it's not going to be smooth as you would like it to be all the time, but don't let obstacles stop you. Don't be afraid to take that chance today, you have nothing to lose.

or believing in me.

Life Growing Up in Tobago

My Home Life

As we know, Trinidad and Tobago is a twin-island country, of which Tobago is the smaller of the two islands. My life growing up in Tobago was good, but it had its challenges. My mother, my guardian Burt, Kimone, my cousin, and my grandmother, all played a significant role in assisting me with developing my moral values. They taught me the importance of staying focused, maintaining respect for elders, demonstrating good manners, and more. At Thirty years of age and looking back on my life, I have nothing but gratitude to them for helping me build a good foundation for my life and for always motivating me to achieve my goals. Without them helping me to build a solid foundation, I would not have been the person I am today.

Being Part of an Extended Family

The family I grew up in was what is termed an extended

family, meaning that my household also included cousins, aunts, uncles, grandmother, and grandfather. When my mother was out working additional jobs for extra money to provide for us, my cousin Kimone, along with my grandmother and Burt, took care of my sisters and me.

My mother would always give Kimone money to take us shopping and to attend activities such as Carnival Monday and Tuesday parades, Easter Crab and Goat Races, and the Great Race weekend activities which occur each year in Tobago. I fondly remember that my sister, Kimika, and I, would always wear the same outfit, just different colors, because with our birthdays being August 27th and 28th one year and a day apart, we could have been likened to twins. Kimone loved us like we were her own children and I am also very thankful to her for all the knowledge she has passed on and all the assistance she rendered, that helped my sisters and me become the great women we are today.

My aunt, Patsy, and she and her husband, whom we called Slim, have been steadfast in supporting us with our football activities and other endeavours. They were always among the first people to see us on the News and tell everyone that we were on the television, or to cut out our pictures when we appeared in the newspapers, photographed with the national team.

Village Life

In Tobago, we grew up in a village called Plymouth. It was a neighborhood that was at times, challenged by drugs, violence, and other negative activities. The police would sometimes be out in the village searching for drug dealers. Since this environment was what it was, I did what I had to do to ensure that I created a better life for myself. I recall that in my younger days, my mother would require us to be inside our home by six o'clock on evenings during the school term so that we could do our homework and prepare for school the next day. On weekends I would usually meet up with neighbourhood friends to engage in fun activities. Some of these activities included: cricket, basketball, football, hopscotch, rounders, moral, marble pitching, piggy in the middle, hide and seek, catching, and rubber band texts. I would long for weekends to come so that I could be allowed to go outside and play with my neighbours. As I grew older, I was able to earn more privileges, and at age eighteen I was permitted to go to the mall with friends and to the beach on my own. Plymouth was always a very active place with much to do, and it is this that caused me to recognise from an early age that I needed to maintain my focus on achieving my academic and career goals.

In hindsight, I realise that even though there was often a negative stigma attached to Plymouth and its residents, this never deterred me from striving to achieve my goals. On the contrary, the environment motivated me to prove to the naysayers that good things could come out of the village of Plymouth. Though some people may still refer to my beloved hometown as the "ghetto", the village can boast of producing a few other successful athletes, apart from me. These individuals include Daniel Cyrus - a pro footballer, Rundell Winchester - a pro footballer, Mark London - an athlete, and Kellyanne Baptiste, one of Trinidad and Tobago's most prolific track and field sprint athletes. Thus, it is evident that in spite of the negative stigma attached to the village, Plymouth has borne some good fruit.

Also on the flip side of the negatives, Plymouth has four beautiful beaches and was once home to the Tobago Jazz Festival and has therefore witnessed the presence of a few world-renowned artistes. Plymouth also houses the Mystery Tombstone which is one of Tobago's most popular tourist attractions. Plymouth is also home to its very own steel orchestra and it has been successful four years in a row. Among all of the village Heritage Festival shows, Plymouth is proud to host one of the most anticipated and well-attended shows on the island.

So great is my love for my village and for giving back to my community, that in 2014 I started a football tournament which I named "Kick it with Karyn". I felt that as someone who is thought to be a well-respected person in the community I should use the influence I possess to create more positives in the community. The tournament "Kick it with Karyn", a football competition in which teams compete against each other in a bid to win money and other prizes. Apart from football, there are other activities which also happen on the day of the tournament, such as All Fours matches for the adults and Bouncy Castle and other fun activities for the children. In my assessment of the tournament and its effectiveness at achieving the goals I had in mind at its inception, I can safely say that it impacts the community in a very positive way, bringing members of the community together and engaging them in activities that are uplifting and enjoyable, and for me that's great. I must say that being able to do this tournament is a great joy, especially seeing the community members being involved on a yearly basis. By keeping the tournament annually, it encourages the youths to have something to look forward to and to engage in something positive.

It pleases me greatly to see that in Plymouth we are becoming more developed, now having more positive activities being initiated by individuals such as Donneal Vincent, who does strength and fitness training coupled with some aerobics at the field in Plymouth. Thus there are more methods through which people can stay constructively occupied and away from trouble. There is a need for more positive influences, and additional activities that can further create a more positive outlook is exactly what the village needs. I hope to continue to do more things to create a positive change within the community. By doing this the younger generation would have a less hostile environment in which to grow up.

Tobago Cuisine

In Tobago, we are very family-oriented people, and I have learnt many things while living at home in Plymouth with my extended family. Due to the foundation that was instilled in me from my mother and other family members, it was mandatory as a young lady to learn how to cook meals, clean the house, wash clothes and maintain proper personal hygiene. However, learning how to cook was a major priority. There was no set age but once you were at an age where you were able to learn, you would have been taught to cook. These lessons could have been given by your mother, grandmother, aunts, it didn't matter whom, you would be summoned to come and learn. These elder ladies, my mother most of all, always said, "When you have a husband and he puts you in house, you have to be able to provide for your family." Yes, we Tobagonians eat fast food but many prefer to cook their natural foods the majority of the time. To this day I do not like buying food. I prefer home-cooked food, simply because it's healthier, it's cheaper and I can still hear my mother's words echoing in my mind.

You had to be able to cook multiple dishes and your training began with mastering the simple stewed chicken and rice, pasta and corned beef, saltfish and dumplings, and fried fish and provision. When you were proficient at creating these simple dishes, you would then advance to one of our favorite dishes in Trinidad and Tobago, "Pelau", which is comprised of rice, cooked with carrot, peas, corn, garlic, ginger, celery, etc and then advanced dishes such as macaroni pie, curried chicken, callaloo, potato salad, fish bread, fried bake, roasted bake and more. Of course, everyone knows that Trinidad's "sister isle", Tobago, is known for its delectable "crab and dumpling". Haaa! It's true! Therefore this was one of the dishes you had to learn to cook. We love to cook dumplings with different meats. For example, dumplings can go with pork, stewed chicken, goat, iguana, fish, corned beef, and saltfish. It just depends on how you feel on a particular day. In Tobago, we often refer to cooking as the art of "flicking your risk".

Growing up in Tobago our parents encouraged the use of more natural foods such as ground provision - sweet potatoes, cassava, dasheen, yam, and other provisions such as plantain and green figs, to name a few. Most people say when you are from Tobago, you are known to be strong and healthy individuals because of the natural foods that you eat, and at the ages of thirteen and fourteen, my sister and I were huge, because of our Tobago diet. When we first arrived on the national team, we were two of the biggest girls on the team, if not the biggest. Our physical strength came from having a solid foundation of "blue food", which is thought to be healthy food.

Chapter 1

The Start of My Football Journey

At the tender age of five, I started playing football with Stokley Vale FC, the club based in my village of Plymouth. The field on which we trained was located within walking distance of my home. As a youth growing up, I played most of my football with boys because at the onset of my career, there weren't many girls playing football in my community, it was mainly my sister and me. I enjoyed playing with boys because it helped me improve my game in numerous ways. I became more physical, and I learned to play faster than when I played with girls. The years I spent playing with boys created a competitive environment. They helped me with developing mental toughness, improving my physicality and my technical ability, thereby causing my game to improve tremendously. I was classified as a "tomboy" playing among the boys, but I didn't care, because I knew one day, I would become successful at playing football. Today I can boast of being able to play in any position on the football field except in that of a goalkeeper. My favorite positions are midfield and the "stopper" position which is in the defense.

The coach who is responsible for me developing into the player I am today is James Campbell, better known as "Flabby". Under his tutelage at the Stokley Vale FC Academy, I developed most of my football skills. James is an excellent coach, we had done a great amount of one on one sessions, helping my football skills and improving my game tremendously. James even bought me my first pair of football shoes. He has supported me throughout my career and he is the one who I will always credit for getting me to where I am and for whom I would always have great respect.

My game continued to develop over the years because, with every opportunity I got, I would be playing and practising the game with my cousins and neighbors. My sister and I were the only girls but that did not deter us, and that helped us to become better players. In the early days, my sister was a field player; it took a year for her to decide that she was stronger in the goalkeeping position. She is actually really good at it today. Both my sister and I went on to play primary and secondary level school football, then furthered our careers at the national level. We took our careers to another level, both securing scholarships and then playing at the college level. Later on, we both got the opportunity to play professionally. My sister played in Paraguay then she settled in Colombia and is now playing at a high level. As for me, I got my first contract last year, 2019, in Iceland, which I would discuss later on in the book.

In my early days of playing football, there weren't any avenues for female players at the youth level, so I played my first competitive tournament in the Republic Cup Tournament for boys. in the category, Youth 12 and Under Boys, as the only girl. I performed so well that I won the "Most Valuable Player" (MVP) award because I scored the winning goal in the finals. There and then, I decided that I would continue to take football seriously. I trained every Saturday with those boys and also did beach training, two Saturdays of every month. Some of my strengths as a player include the ability to kick the ball with both legs hard, I am very "rugged", I can read the game well and I have a lot of vision in finding a player to score. I am strong on the ball and it's very difficult to bounce me off the ball. I am a dead ball specialist, having been the dead-ball specialist on all the club teams and national teams that I have played for thus far in my career. Approximately 95% of my goals are scored from outside the 18-yard box. This is because I can really strike the ball well with both feet. All of these qualities were gained from being coached by James, and training and playing among boys which Coach James always recommended.

Though playing with boys was not easy, it worked well and served to produce many positives, of which I continue to reap the benefits. One of my strengths is that I am always willing to train and work hard and this has significantly contributed to the success I have been able to enjoy in my career thus far. My work ethic is what I used to let my talent in football channel my life in the direction where I am able to accomplish any goals that I set. The exposure from travelling to many different countries because of football has not only impacted my development as a player but also as a person. My advice to any young person, who may be talented in a sporting discipline, is to believe in yourself, put in the work, and watch your hard work pay off. Football carried me to places I never thought I would see and I often look back and smile, because I have come a long way, a pertinent reminder of the reason I named this book "Woman of Substance". It identifies the various aspects of my life that have contributed to my success, including football, my life experiences, family, and mentorship from elders or people I confide in. They all served to help me blossom into a "Woman of Substance".

Chapter 2

Playing Football at the Primary and Secondary School Levels

As mentioned above, I mainly played with males in the early period of my football career. I then got my opportunity to play in my first female competition with Bethesda Government Primary School. It was a great experience, and there is where I knew I was destined for greatness. Playing at the primary school level earned me recognition and it helped me to be scouted by one of the top secondary schools in Tobago - Signal Hill Secondary School. In the early part of my career, I did not take my academics seriously. All I wanted to do was play football. I did not become more diligent with my academics until I completed the Secondary Entrance Assessment (SEA). My results were poor. I had passed for Goodwood High School, which was considered to be one of the lower performing secondary schools in

Tobago. It was there and then that reality hit me. All of my friends had passed for the top three schools in Tobago and they were celebrating with their parents, while I was left feeling like I had let my mother and family down. I felt hopeless!

As a result of my being a promising footballer, Mrs. Simons got me transferred to Signal Hill Senior Comprehensive school which was touted as the second-best performing school in Tobago. Signal Hill was a really good "football" school, and there my talent in football saw me through. Admittedly, even though I had secured a transfer to Signal Hill Senior Comprehensive school, I still did not take my academics as seriously as I should have; my focus continued to be on playing football. I did complete my academics, but I wasn't as devoted to it as I should have been. Instead, I was more passionate about football and that's where I placed the bulk of my effort.

Playing at the secondary school level made me even more popular where football was concerned. Over the years I amassed more than seven individual football awards and helped my school win the Secondary School League three times in a row. While I was a part of the team, we travelled to Trinidad and won the Intercol Championship twice playing against St. Augustine Secondary School and Malick Secondary School respectively. My main focus then was on playing football, finishing school, and playing professionally.

As we know, the high school experience culminates with each student completing an exam set by the Caribbean Examination Council, which depending on one's performance in the various subject areas, can qualify one to fill entry-level positions in several jobs. After completing the exam, I had passed two subjects: Principles of Accounts with a grade two and Physical Education with a grade one. Having sat a total of six subjects and passed two, I had therefore failed four subjects. It was at this point that it hit home that I had been playing the fool in school and had placed too much emphasis on football and not enough on my academics. Like my grandmother would say, I needed a good "cut tail". What bothered me the most about my results, was the fact that my mother had always ensured that my sisters and I had all the necessities for school, so that we could excel. My mother's obvious disappointment caused me to speak seriously to myself about there being life apart from football and that I needed to do better.

Thankfully, because of the way the system is designed whereby students are sometimes offered a chance to repeat the subjects which they had failed, and because I played football and could have still represented my school, I was granted the opportunity to do the subjects again. My guardian, Burt, who loved me like a father, believed in me and knew that I could have done better, helped me by paying for extra lessons for both Mathematics and English.

Those two subjects were the subjects that I had struggled with the most, and so I focused on them a bit more. I did the classes with an old school teacher, Mrs. Lyons. Her classes were small so I was able to receive the attention needed to be successful at the exams.

Chapter 3

Attending University in the United States of America

I attended two different universities in the United States of America. The first University was Northwood University in Dallas, Texas. When I earned the scholarship to both universities respectively, this is when I decided that I would need to get serious about my academics. Obviously, I knew that university is higher education and I would need to apply myself much more diligently to be able to balance both academics and football. My first weeks in college were a bit challenging because I was homesick and I missed my family and friends, but I knew that I would have eventually had to adjust to the lifestyle and adapt to the different culture.

At Northwood University, I had to try to settle as quickly as I could, while being open to meeting new people, and adjusting to climate change as well. There were four other persons from Trinidad and Tobago who attended Northwood University as well. It's always difficult being away from home, but having other student-athletes from my home country at the same school helped me to get adjusted quickly. With there being so few of us Trinbagonians, we stuck together and over time we all became good friends. The thing about college is that even though you may not have known a particular person from your home country prior to attending college, once you both end up in the same school or environment, you automatically become close regardless of the other friends you may make along the way.

When I was leaving for the States, I had the notion that I needed to be tough and take no nonsense from anyone. This was my mindset because of what I had heard of other people's experiences. In spite of that, I still felt the need to gain my own experience of American culture and college life. I marvelled that the United States of America is such a large country and I was excited to experience what it was like to live in a developed country and learn how they operate on all levels. It was amazing to me to see how they take their sports very seriously. The United States academic system is also really good. Besides the culture, I got a chance to meet some really wonderful people on this journey at both universities and I was able to build friendships that will last for a lifetime.

Coming back to my preconceived notions about life at U.S. universities, I can remember quite well, two situations in which I had found myself while attending Northwood. Both incidents occurred on the football field with two girls on the team. The first incident happened because when new players arrive, of course, everyone would be watching to see how talented you are and to assess the likelihood of you taking their spot on the team. There was this one Brazilian girl , who felt she was the "female Marta", hahaha! When I saw her play and knowing my ability, I felt that she wasn't ready for me. Lol! As soon as I started to play, I stamped my authority immediately, and my quality as a player was obvious. Apparently, she didn't like that and when we both got into a collision, she straight up kicked me. I got up and kicked her right back! Remember, because of the notion I had, I wasn't about to back down. I actually earned respect from her after that incident. Lol! In the second altercation, a player named Liz became irate when I tackled her; one of my strengths as a footballer is the fact that I can tackle really hard, so I tackled Liz and she got upset. She decided to retaliate by calling me the "B" word. You know that would get anyone mad, so I said to her, I am not a lady of talk; I am a woman of action, lol. She kept talking and I advised her that she was wasting my time with her chatter. As punishment for going at each other, the coach sent us both to run laps. After that incident, we knew that we had to play on the same team so we adopted the attitude of teammates rather than rivals. I went on to dominate during my first season, making it on the all-star team and scoring a number of goals.

Having become accustomed to being in a competitive environment, I knew I had to endure certain situations and that that's where my true strength would be evident. I learnt that you would encounter many different situations on your journey, some of them unpleasant and trying, but be wise about the decisions you choose to make. Following those incidents, I got to realize that not every battle is meant for you to fight. Going through those situations really helped me to mature and I am thankful, for they helped my growth as a Woman of Substance on this life's journey. Lesson learnt, choose your battles wisely!

Chapter 4

COLLEGE CULTURE SHOCK
SOCCER VS FOOTBALL

In Trinidad and Tobago, we say "football" and in the United States they say "soccer". Football in the United States is considered "American Football". Upon my arrival in the U.S, I felt a bit culture-shocked about "football" being called "soccer", because it was a new term for me being different from what I was accustomed to in Trinidad and Tobago. Even the playing format in college for "soccer" was set up differently, and it was interesting to see how the college system worked.

First, in order to play in the United States, foreigners have to go through something called the "clearinghouse". The clearinghouse is essentially a background check, ensuring that you did not play professionally or engage in any activities that could jeopardize your eligibility. If the background check showed that you played professionally, this could result in you losing eligibility. The length of time you were allowed to play in college is 4 years, so the eligibility center would determine how many years you gain or lose depending on the situation. For example, any leagues that you have participated in had to be amateur leagues in order for you not to lose your eligibility. Two of the main organizing bodies that most students may have gone through would have been the National Collegiate Athletic Association (NCAA) and the National Association of Intercollegiate Athletics (NIAIA) at the university level. There is also, junior college level, which students often used as an avenue to get into the school system. Junior college is basically two years, then one could move on to the university level for the remaining two years.

To attend university as an international student, you have to take the Scholastic Aptitude Test (SAT). There would be a required score based on each university's standard. Junior college has its own requirements. At the junior college level, you do not need to complete the SAT. It's a quicker system and many choose that route for that reason. University standards are higher since there is the SAT, while for junior college you simply need to do Mathematics and English entrance tests to get admitted. The rules for entry into university are strict and the clearinghouse process could be pretty long, hence the reason many opt to attend junior college first then transfer. Both NAIA and NCAA have many rules and procedures and the process can be frustrating but it is worth it in the end.

Soccer is ranked highly among the sports played in the United States. They have one of the most recognized colleges' leagues on all levels worldwide. Many international students travel from all over the world, leaving their countries and migrating to the United States to earn their degrees, but moreover, to play soccer and other sports competitively at the university level.

Now the United States is becoming more diverse. In the colleges' league, players are able to win yearly awards and play more than 18 games. Once the team advances to the regional tournaments, they can play even more games. As they advance, the teams enjoy the luxuries of winning trophies, conference rings, weekly awards, regional awards, academic awards, and other accolades.

To mention a bit of what happens before the games, the United States' anthem plays before every college game, in spite of the level. Each soccer game usually lasts ninety minutes. The timer would stop if there is an injury. In doing so, the referees do not have to give extra time. There are unlimited substitutions but with one restriction, if a player exited the field during the first half of the game, the player isn't allowed to re-enter the game until the second half. In the second half, the player can come in and go out of the game without any restrictions. In college, we played regular games where it did not matter if we won or lost, but it was good to win to keep our record good at the end of the season. The conference games were the important games that we had to ensure we won. If at the end of the game, the score was tied, then match officials would proceed by having us play extra time. The team that scored within the extra time, would have won the game. If no team had scored at the end of extra time, then the points were shared. This is what makes extra time fun but scary at the same time. The leagues were very competitive. At the end of the season, the coaches would vote on various players to determine who should receive individual awards such as the all-conference team which recognises the best eleven players for the season, striker of the season, midfielder of the season, defender of the season and goalkeeper of the season. This system repeats every year, so you have the opportunity to receive these awards annually until your eligibility is over.

At the end of your playing career in college, there is something called "senior day". Senior day is your last home game, and before you play that game, you usually get a chance to hear your overall stats for the last four years of your college career, minutes played, and other achievements. Senior day sometimes leads to tears from players and coaches because it signifies that the bonds created at that level have more or less come to an end. Now you have to move on with your life into the real world. Though you would still keep in contact with coaches and players with whom you built friendships, the reality is that chapter of your life is over. I can safely say that when you are finished playing those four years, I can safely say you now have many memories to cherish.

Chapter 5

My Second Stop
Transferring to West Texas

The second university I attended was West Texas A&M University, located in Texas, in a small town called Canyon. I must mention that Charleston University in South Carolina was actually my first choice. However, when I communicated with the coach at Charleston, I was not entirely comfortable, so I had second thoughts about going there. West Texas A&M was my second choice so I decided to talk to the coach, Chad Webb. Immediately, after speaking with Coach Webb, I knew that West Texas was my choice. Rhea Belgrave, my best friend, made my choice easier because she was already attending West Texas. Throughout my time at West Texas, I was able to make new friends, work alongside new teammates, benefit from the expertise of new coaches and make memories that I would cherish forever. At West Texas A&M, I completed my Bachelor's degree in Business Administration and then went on to further my studies by doing my Master's Degree in Interdisciplinary Studies, with a concentration in Counselling, Communication, and Management. Initially, I had no intention of pursuing a Masters but I was granted the opportunity and I made the best use of it. While completing my Master's degree, I was able to gain knowledge that enhanced my perspective from an educational standpoint. West Texas was also known to be one of the best schools, not only with athletics but academically, ranked in Texas at the Division Two level. Unlike Northwood which is an all-business school, West Texas was far more advanced, and they had a wider curriculum from which one could choose a range of degrees.

In my second season abroad and my first season at West Texas, I was injured and was forced to sit out most of the season. At the start of the third season, I was healed, fit, and ready to push myself. During that season I scored over 8 goals, along with picking up the award for being one of the Best Eleven players in the Conference, also earning Division Two All-region awards. It was a great year to build on and it gave me more confidence to try to achieve additional goals for the final year of my college career. In the final year of my four seasons, I again made the Best Eleven conference team and secured multiple Division Two All-region awards. To add to my awards that year, I earned midfielder of the year 2016 in the conference. West Texas also won the conference in 2016. It was a pretty successful year, and I was able to win a ring before I ended my college career.

I enjoyed the experience at both schools, with Northwood University being a National Association of Intercollegiate Athletics (NAIA) and West Texas school being a National Collegiate Athletic Association (NCAA). West Texas was a much bigger school, with more opportunities, while Northwood was a private and smaller school. I didn't have any altercations with any of the players at West Texas, they were very cool and I felt more welcomed. Coach Chad Webb, my coach at that time, was a really nice person. He cared about his players on and off the field. I helped Coach Webb to recruit other Trinidad and Tobago-born players for the team after I had completed my years of eligibility. A few of those players were Shanelle Arjoorn, Khadisha and Khadidra Debesette, Asha James, and Khaline Jacob. I must say that my college experience was great. I was able to gain first-hand experience in a diverse environment. I would always encourage anyone to attend college and further their education if they get the chance. Note that everyone's experience would be different; you have to do it yourself and gain your own experience.

Being away from home is not easy but sometimes an opportunity presents itself leaving you with no choice but to go further afield. In everything that we do, there would be pros and cons. I knew that whatever career path I chose, I had to ensure I made something of myself because I needed to help my mother. I had seen my mother work hard to ensure I have the necessary tools, so I wanted to return the favor by earning my degree, giving her something to be proud of, and letting her see that all her hard work did not go to waste. In the first couple of years, I made the "Dean's List". My GPA was 3.5 and up, and I even received an academic certificate. I know I had to balance both my athletics and academics because, in the event, I went under a 2.0 GPA, I would have been unable to play football and would have been placed on academic probation. I was very serious with school, I attended all my classes, I did all my homework, and studied for exams. In the end, it all was paying off because my GPA was a solid 3.0. I was on top of things. I was very disciplined. Sometimes, we travelled for 8 hours and more to play away games, and there were times we also left school during the week to play games, which caused me to miss classes. I had to manage my time well. I was keeping in touch with professors or other students in my class to send assignments, notes, etc. Knowing where I came from and having done so well with my academics, makes me feel a great sense of pride.

College gives you a different outlook on life. I needed this stage in my life which did nothing more than build my character and helped shape me into the person I am today. As I aged and matured, my ultimate goal was always to grow into a "woman of substance".

Chapter 6

Balancing Athletics and Academics

Being able to balance athletics and academics wasn't always easy, but it was worth it in the end. I spent long hours daily in the library, getting assignments done and studying for exams. The library personnel became very familiar with me and knew me by name, because of the number of hours I spent there. My schedule was: go to class in the mornings, then to the library for four hours, after which I would go grab my gear and head to football practice. When practice ended, I would shower and go back to the library for another three to four hours. As the time drew closer to finals, my hours spent in the library increased.

One of the hardest times to balance both athletics and academics was when the team had 'away' games when we travelled for long hours on a bus but still had to ensure that our assignments were completed on time. At those times, I would often communicate with my professors via email, about assignments or any other material I needed for class or exams. Being able to balance both athletics and academics, helped me to become disciplined, practice good time management skills, good organizational skills and it also helped me develop character. I can safely say that this process of having to balance athletics and academics, helped me positively in so many areas of my life. Partying was never my thing so I was very focused. I didn't have any reasons to allow that aspect to factor into my routine in college.

The knowledge that I have gained during the years in college has really humbled me. In addition, my degree in Business Management facilitated the acquisition of many new skills and ways in which to orchestrate and run a business. It is my intention to further utilise the motivation and discipline derived from balancing athletics and academics to start my own business in the future because besides sports, I am very passionate about business. I have already opened my store, "FFVC APPAREL" and I also launched my new clothing line on that same day, January 1st, 2020.

Throughout my life, I have learnt that achievements do not always have to be physical. To many, being able to balance both athletics and academics may not seem like a big achievement, but it is for me. I think it's these types of overlooked victories that usually teach us lifelong lessons. In college, I was able to accept the responsibility of balancing those two very important areas of my life and gain independence by having a place of my own, cooking for myself, paying bills, and more. College helped me to adopt good problem-solving skills and forced me to weigh options to make good decisions.

One thing I struggled with in the earlier part of my college career, was being homesick, but both my coach, Chad Webb, and his wife Joy Webb, always made me feel welcomed and at home. They both would go out of their way to make me feel comfortable. Even though my stint at West Texas has ended, I remain grateful to them for their hospitality, love, and support and I still keep in touch with them from time to time. I love them like my own parents as they were there every step of the way along my college journey and I thank them for that every chance I get.

Balancing athletics and academics for four years is not an easy task, but once you put your mind to it and focus, you can do it. There would certainly be challenging times, but these times can make you stronger and propel you to push through to the end. I am very happy that I pushed myself beyond my initial expectations and used these experiences to help me to reach my ultimate goal. This was just another journey I had to endure in my quest to grow into a "woman of substance".

Chapter 7

DISTRACTIONS IN COLLEGE

In college, there is every and anything you could think about that can distract you. First of all, you are living on your own, so you are making your own decisions and for many, the novelty of having such freedom can lead to a host of poor choices. Nothing is wrong with having fun and exploring new people, new activities on campus, and other things in which you would like to engage yourself during college. However, on the flip side of that is while having fun, you have to understand if those fun aspects are causing you to lose focus, you have to be smart and start to make adjustments to regain your focus. In the event you lose focus, you have to eliminate those entities that are causing you to lose focus. It's a case where you have to settle down again and create a timetable to enable you to better manage your time. At the top of your schedule, you need to place your priorities while your extra-curricular activities should come toward the end. I understand that having completed your four years of college, you want to have created a myriad of great memories upon which you can reminisce, but you also need to keep your "eye on the prize". Your ultimate goal, when you leave college, ought to be to ensure that you have successfully completed your degree. As a student-athlete, you have to be able to balance your extra-curricular activities, your academics, and sports. You know yourself best, and in the event, you feel like you are getting off track, you have to immediately rein yourself in and get back on course.

A few of the main distractions in college come immediately to mind - college parties, hanging out with the wrong crowd, smoking, breaking university rules, irresponsibly partaking of alcohol, missing class, and engaging carelessly in sexual activity. As I said previously, parties weren't my thing, but everyone's vice is different. If you're going to have fun, know your limits! When the freedom associated with college life threatens your academic focus, you have to be responsible enough to know that being in college and living on your own are setting the tone for your future by providing you with practice in making wise decisions. Do not fall into that trap of wanton freedom! Be smart! My advice is to have fun but be smart while doing it!

Being an international student on a full scholarship, you need to exercise greater effort to not be stupid and getting carried away by the luxuries and freedom in college. There is much more at stake for us as internationals, because getting a full scholarship is always a plus for us. Some of our parents cannot afford to pay for college. Overall, create a balance and utilize your time wisely. Life is there to enjoy, doing things that you love, but you also have to be logical and wise about your decisions.

I think college is a great test and experience for a person going away from home and being on one's own in a different country. It truly builds you as a person. However, in order to gain these positive results, you have to make good decisions. College usually gives you a little bit of everything, it challenges you, it motivates you, it develops you in positive ways, but it can affect you negatively if you are reckless. Distractions are usually there to present different trials, to see how focused you are on achieving your goals. You just have to decide your destiny and act in a manner that would ensure the realisation of your goals. Every decision you make can affect you either negatively or positively, so this is why I would urge everyone to be wise. Your future lies in your hands, but it can easily be thwarted by distractions. Do not fall victim to them. Accept the opportunity of experiencing everything college has to offer but demonstrate astuteness in your decision making. At the end of your four years, ensure that you are one of the students throwing your hat up in the air. Don't be that student, who has been in university for five, six years, continuing to struggle to reach that elusive milestone.

Chapter 8

Humorous College Moments

In college, there were so many hilarious moments, but unfortunately, I can only speak about a few. One moment that I will never forget, is the moment I became aware of the tradition in college, where once you are a freshman, you have the responsibility of carrying the bag of balls to training. One of the seniors, a girl in her final year, wanted the freshmen to carry the balls. The seniors usually liked to give orders because in college that is one of the privileges they are allowed. Though I was a freshman, I knew I wasn't about to carry no balls. Knowing my ability and my Trinbago culture of not liking to be bullied, I simply kept my face serious, and so, no one told me anything. In hindsight, I think I was not pressured to perform that particular task because I was a good player. Lol! I had been awaiting the moment when I would be asked to take the balls to the field, but it never came, and looking back, I am happy it never happened.

Another incident I encountered occurred when we were off to a game and there was this one senior with a really bad attitude; as previously mentioned, I was a freshman at the time. We were travelling to an "away" college game and when she boarded the bus, she straight up said to me, "Freshmen get up, I need a seat". Well, you know Karyn was not moving, because I knew she couldn't have been speaking to me. There were some other freshmen sitting alongside me, and she walked up to one of them and told her to get up. I think she did not say anything to me because I was watching her dead in her face, waiting for her to utter a word to me. I was ready to unleash a verbal attack on her. Haha!

Yet another interaction I will not forget was with another girl. At first, we couldn't see eye to eye, but we are really good friends today. Natile was one of the better players on the team at my first school, Northwood University. When the coach introduced us I was very cold because prior to my arrival I had received the information that she could play but she had an attitude. From that moment I decided that she would be one from whom I would maintain my distance. We were always competing against each other on the field, which was not always a good thing. We both were talented players and we were quite aware of this, and so we didn't have much to do with each other sticking to our ways and nurturing our egos. What caused the turn, bringing us together, was the one class we had together - History. We were forced to communicate because we needed to get some information for class and so our first conversation was initiated. We had to put our differences aside for the sake of the academic success of us both and in so doing we became friends. After that first conversation, I realized that she was not that bad after all.

Looking back at the early days when we refused to even speak with each other, seems so strange because we have become really good friends and that friendship still lives on today. Now we look back and laugh about our past encounters, especially our battles on the field to prove which one of us was the better player. One lesson I have learnt is that it's important to form your own opinions of people instead of listening to others. I now realise that it is beneficial to engage in healthy battles, but at the end of the day, you must be able to find peace with your teammates regardless. Realistically speaking it's always going to be competitive when you become a part of a new team but you have to rise to the challenge and conquer it, no matter the environment. Positivity always, remember that throughout life.

But wait, I am not yet done recounting the humorous moments at my first college. At Northwood University, the mall was a couple of hours' walk but a five-minute drive from the school. My friend, Sharice, a fellow Trinbagonian, and I, sometimes rode our bikes to the mall to do some shopping and there were a few times that we walked as well. We liked to take advantage of the weekend sales, but since we had no transportation, we had to be innovative. I recall that on those occasions when we would walk to the mall people would look at us like we were crazy. Haha! They were probably asking themselves who were these crazy ladies randomly walking on the streets. Our biggest target for shopping was the "Black Friday Sale". We did not care how we got to the mall, whether it was walking, riding, asking for a ride, and finding our way back, we were determined to get there. We made up our minds that we were not missing the "Black Friday Sale"! The good thing was that it was always the two of us, so we had each other's company to "old talk" on our way to or from the mall. Sometimes if we walked to the mall, we would wait outside the mall, to ask for a lift back to school because after shopping we would often have too many bags to carry. That was funny because our getaway slang was, "we are internationals and have no cars". Honestly, many people have fallen for the slang, even though the slang was the truth. People often felt sorry for us and we never once got rejected, thank God for that. That was an adventure that I would always look back on and laugh.

Apart from Sharice and me, there was another girl from Trinidad and Tobago named Shanelle. During our off-season, we managed to find a Mexican league with which to play, and in that league, we played for Real Madrid; the teams used professional football names, such as Barcelona, Real Madrid, etc. Barcelona was the top team in the league, they had good players, and on our team were the three "Trinbagonians", the best players on the team. We knew we would have eventually had to play Barcelona which was the strongest team in the competition.

Finally, that day came to play, Barcelona versus us, Real Madrid. This game was a "clash of titans". From the moment the game started, the heat was on. The game was very physical. The Barcelona team realized that they weren't dominating the game so they started to throw unnecessary punches and kicks. The referee wasn't doing a good job and so, the game got out of hand. I was playing in the defensive midfield position and I was doing well, but one of the girls from the Barcelona team started to play me really dirty. The slogan among Sharice, Shanelle, and I had always been, "you hit one, you hit all". On one occasion when the girl gave me an underhanded tackle I fell to the ground. I remember seeing Sharice, who is 5'1", fly in with a jump kick! HaaHaa! It was at that moment that the drama started and the field filled with members of both teams and the spectators who had been backing each side, going at each other. We immediately began looking for a way out because the situation was fast becoming brutal. Shanelle, Sharice, and I took up our gear and started sprinting to the car to leave the area because those Mexicans were furious. We never played in that area again. The team was just upset because we went a goal up and they were accustomed to winning the league. From the moment they realized that they weren't going to win the game and more than likely win the league, they started getting very hostile.

Even though that incident proved to be quite scary, it was really a moment that we enjoyed being a bit naughty. It's common knowledge that we Trinibagonian people like to "give talk" or taunt, so honestly, we did torture them a bit, giving them some chats here and there during the game. Lol! I guess they did not like that very much.

I cherish such memories because I think it's wonderful to not just look back and laugh, but to remember any lessons that I may have learnt along the way. I also think that these memories would make great stories to tell my children in the future.

Chapter 9

NATIONAL CAREER

I started playing with Trinidad and Tobago's national team from age thirteen. I was recruited while playing in an Intercol final. I attended Signal Hill Senior Comprehensive in Tobago, and it was Signal Hill vs Malick Secondary. Some of the girls from Malick were already on the national team and when they saw me play, they told the then national coach, Jamal Shabazz, about me. He later contacted me to visit Trinidad to try out for the team. Coach Shabazz was impressed when he saw me play and he wanted me to continue training with the team which helped me to later gain a permanent spot on the team.

There were a few other Tobagonian players on the team - my sister Kimika Forbes, Kenya Cordner, Julianne Mc Dougal, Jossane Bois, and Candice Edwards. My first selection for the national team was when we traveled to Venezuela, to play a few friendly matches against the Venezuelan national women's team. It was then that I made my debut with the T&T national team, playing in the two games against Venezuela, both of which we won. Now at Thirty

years old, I am still a part of the team, still playing and continuing to dominate.

I can definitely say that playing nationally, exposed me to a range of experiences that helped me grow as a person and further developed my football career. National caps helped me to earn both a scholarship to study in the United States of America and to secure my first professional contract in Iceland. Having the experience of playing nationally, really helps your game and it opens up doors for scholarships and professional clubs.

Throughout my years of playing on the national team, I have travelled to many other countries courtesy of football. I have set foot on the shores of Colombia, St Lucia, Barbados, England, Hawaii, Mexico, Canada, the United States, Venezuela, and many other countries. One thing I liked about travelling with the national team, was being able to see different countries. Travelling exposed me to many things such as new cultures, scenery, lifestyle, sports, etc, and opened my eyes to issues such as poverty.

During my tenure with the T&T national team, I have played in all the age groups, Youth 17, Youth 20, and at the senior level. Over the years of playing with the national team, Trinidad and Tobago has been known as one of the powerhouses in the Caribbean but the CONCACAF level is where we usually struggle. A few of the teams which usually pose a challenge to us are the United States, Canada, Mexico, and Costa Rica, mainly because they have better resources and they are always a bit more prepared going into competitions. Additionally, the players on these teams are players in some of the top professional leagues, and their developmental programs and leagues are very organized. Contrarily, we usually struggle to prepare because of limited resources and not enough opportunities to play international games. Therefore, we are always at a disadvantage.

Another major positive of playing nationally is the fact that I have been able to witness firsthand and contribute to an improvement in the level of play. Over the years, we have gotten better and we have been closing the gap between our team and those at the top tiers, and we have shown that we can compete well at the CONCACAF level. With every qualifier, we have become more recognized at the CONCACAF level and we got really close to qualifying for the finals in 2014. Our coaches at the time, Randy Waldrum and his son Ben Waldrum, ensured that we had a great strategy that helped us to close the gap on the big teams, and during that season we were the only Caribbean team to hold the United States, the team ranked number one in the world in that 2014 campaign, to a 1-0 loss. On that day, playing against the United States' team that was composed of players like Abby Wambach, Alex Morgan, Hope Solo, Megan Rapinoe, and other world-class players, the Waldrums cemented their position as two of the best coaches thus far in my career from whose expertise I have benefitted. To this day I remain happy and thankful that I got that opportunity.

Besides losing that first game to the United States, we played both Guatemala and Haiti and won both games. We then advanced out of the group with the United States as the second-best team in that group. At that stage, we had three chances. The first chance was against Costa Rica, in which the game ended at full-time in a 2- all draw and which we later lost on penalties. The second chance was against Mexico and we went 2-1 up before Mexico equalized, and then we lost in overtime 4-2. Our last chance was a home and away game against Ecuador. We played Ecuador in Ecuador and tied the game 0-0. Ecuador tried to use their at-home advantage by having us play at one of their high-altitude fields. Of course, we struggled, and two of our players passed out after the game. That was a nightmare but we made it through and tied the game. The second leg of the game was at home in Trinidad & Tobago, and we played before a sold-out stadium. We played really well and had a number of chances, but we did not capitalize on them until later in the game, and it came back to haunt us. The opposing team got a free kick later in the game. From almost half-line, the girl kicked the ball and it went straight into the back of the net. No one touched the ball. That was one of the hardest moments of my life. I did not want to play football anymore. I felt that moment not only stole our chance to qualify but robbed us of the opportunity to carve a niche for women's football in our country. It was quite tragic for us, and it cut players really deep because Ecuador was no match for us, but we did not take our chances and it made us learn the hard way. I was forced to console myself that God said it wasn't our time.

Going through the 2014 campaign has been the best moment in my national career thus far. In that one game in which we could have qualified for the World Cup, the atmosphere in the stadium was electrifying. Personally, I did not want to disappoint our people. This was the first time in years the stadium was that full. All you could have seen was red, white, and black throughout the stadium. There was music playing, and the "vibes" that we Trinbagonian people so enjoy, was palpable. I saw adults cry after we lost that game. As the final whistle blew, I felt like someone had shot me in my heart with a high-velocity bullet.

I actually wanted to quit football after coming so close to qualifying for the World Cup and getting our hearts broken in literally the last few minutes of the game. That was a tough pill to swallow. It took me about six months to start playing again. I had to resume playing with my school, so I took the season off because I needed time to process everything. The good thing about that was that my college coach and I had a very good understanding, so he allowed me the time off to properly process my emotions. Our season was about to start in two months. I had to get myself moving again.

On the journey of becoming a "woman of substance," these were some of the situations that have helped mold me into a better person and this situation contributed to building my character. I have learnt that no matter how it goes down, I must get up and get going again. As much as my teammates and I beat ourselves up, we had to accept that that was simply not our time because if it were, it would have never passed us. God knows all that He does and we cannot question Him. As I grew into a woman of substance, I knew that disappointments and failure helped me to understand that it was just a setup for new doors to open for the future. I trained myself to always look for positives in all situations that may be deemed negative. Being a woman of substance doesn't mean experiencing only good things, but also being able to find solutions to overcome painful situations.

I am still playing with the national team currently. When would I end playing? I would say, I intend to play as long as I can and while doing so, I am setting up myself to fulfill my future plans.

Chapter 10

Positives About the National Team

During my years playing, being an ambassador of Trinidad and Tobago has been such an honor and privilege. I am proud to represent my country, win, lose or draw. My pores raise every time the national anthem plays before a game. Being able to play in major competitions like World Cup qualifiers or Olympic qualifiers is such an amazing experience. When we travelled to these countries, I was able to learn about different cultures and have so much fun with my teammates, whom I now call my sisters for life. Another positive about the national team is that it has helped me to gain recognition. It's always a great feeling, especially when I'm playing in front of a home crowd, including family and friends.

I have become very self-aware while playing with the national team because there are people who look up to you. I try to ensure that I maintain good conduct and be a good role model to the younger ones. Even random people who would have seen you on the news or have become your fans over the years, look at how you carry yourself. Due to the number of years I have been playing for the national team I have earned a great number of national caps which later helped me gain a scholarship to attend college and a professional contract. I have enjoyed playing against some of the best female footballers in the world today, including Megan Rapinoe, Abby Wambach, Hope Solo, Crystal Dunn, Shannon Boxx, and others. These are some prominent names on the world football stage. These ladies have won more than two World Cups during their careers. Our hardest games would be against these players, but such games have provided me with good experience and I am happy for the opportunity. Currently, my best friend is Rhea Belgrave, having built that relationship from playing Youth 17, Youth 20, and senior-level together.

Throughout the years of being on the national team, another positive has been being coached by multiple coaches, learning their different techniques and tactics, and developing my knowledge of the game of football. Each coach has his own philosophy and techniques, so there is always something to learn from each coach.

Playing with the national team doesn't earn us a salary but we do get a stipend which comes in very handy. My teammates and I love looking forward to our stipend as well as being able to play. Though it isn't much, it helps each of us in many ways. Yes, we have had our challenges playing with the national team but there have been many positives, regardless of some of those tough times. I am very grateful for the opportunity to play with my national team because it has helped me in numerous positive ways.

Chapter 11

Airport Activities; Mentionable Memories

Throughout my twenty-nine years, I have had many memorable moments and if you would indulge me, I would like to mention the one which I hold dear. In one of the earlier chapters, I mentioned that my sister Kimika, Kenya Cordner, Candice Edwards, and I were on the national team together, all originally from Tobago and travelling to Trinidad regularly to train for the national team. I know myself to be more reserved, but the other girls were brave and we would "cause trouble" at the airport. We often tended to get bored when we were at the airport for long hours waiting on a standby flight and that idleness sometimes forced us to give some trouble. I can remember one guy who said he was going to report our behaviour to coach Jamal Shabazz. Most of the time, I was the one to say,

"You all stop!" but deep down, I wanted them to continue because their antics were hilarious.

When the trio, Kenya, Kimika, and Candice, started being mischievous - making jokes and giving people talks, you couldn't help but laugh. Candice especially had a contagious laugh, you don't even have to know what she was laughing about, for you to begin laughing hysterically as well. These girls could brighten up anyone's day! We got to the point where all the airport staff knew us because as we walked up to the desk to check-in, they would just give us a ticket to head home, even if we were on standby. That's just to tell you, how much they wanted to get us out of the airport. Sometimes also, because we were national players representing the country, the service personnel usually sympathized with us and put us on a flight to return home to Tobago to see our families. We were labelled the "trouble makers" at the airport and we were easy to identify because we would always be wearing one of our training tees which boldly stated, "Impossible is Nothing". The tees were faded because of the frequency with which we wore them. Those tees were our favourite training shirts and we would often wash them after practice so that we could wear them again the following day.

At one point we were joined by a fellow Tobagonian who was also selected to travel to Trinidad to train with the national team. She was one of the slowest persons on the field and the way she would position her hand seemed a bit awkward. Candice would be the first one to laugh and like I said this girl's laugh was so contagious that you could not help but burst out laughing as well. We would crack up about it! The new player also wore what we thought were funny shoes, especially when we would go on tour out of the country and were required to wear dress shoes to travel. The coach would tease her by enquiring about where she got her "Nikes" and "Jordans". She would never get upset, always staying so cool, and would often remark, "I am not taking them on at all". In spite of what we thought to be her little quirks, she was a talented player. Screening the ball was one of her greatest strengths; It was not easy to win her ball, and she was also a very technical player.

These experiences taught me about women of substance. The foremost point is that they are not perfect and ought not to ever be aloof. Women of substance have all had silly moments, and have done things that are considered acts of undesirable behaviour. They have also been women who have been kind, generous, supportive, and objective. Perhaps the greatest lesson I learnt during those airport interludes, is that people are entitled to hold any opinion about you that they choose, but it need not define your reality. Never allow what people think of you to change your personality. Even when others may treat you unkindly, maintain your calmness and treat them well. The only person's behaviour for which you are responsible, is yours.

Chapter 12

Playing Professional Football in Iceland

I always wanted to play professional football, so seeing my dreams become a reality made me extremely happy. I felt that once I got that opportunity, there would have been no turning back. Though I know the women's game is not as big as the men's game, I ensured that I equipped myself educationally, in case football did not work out for me. As I mentioned previously, I availed myself of the opportunity to earn two degrees, and in the event of injury, I would have something to fall back on, because there is also life after football. Having a plan B while playing sports is always a plus because life is dynamic and circumstances can change one's course in an instant. I think education is an important factor in anyone's life. Though I know that not everyone would love academics, I would always advise that once the opportunity to engage in study presents itself, one should make the best use of it. For the people who are not academically inclined, I think it's just a matter of finding something you are passionate about and trying to make it into a lucrative enterprise.

Did I envision playing professional football? Yes! Did I think it would have been in Iceland? No! One day while my friend Rhea and I were in Miami on vacation we were talking about life and I was telling her my dream was always to play professional football. I had been praying about my next move in life, and "I said Lord not my will, but Your will". I knew I wanted to play football still so I was just waiting for an opportunity. I did apply for some jobs as well, but deep down I knew that wasn't what I wanted to do. If it had happened though, I would have been happy. I remained patient. A day after having this conversation with my best friend, I got a call from Randy and Ben Waldrum who connected me with an agent, who later got me connected to the team in Iceland. The team was looking for a midfield player who was 5'9" in height. The description of the player they needed, fit me perfectly, and I knew instantly that this opportunity was sent to me from God. I was so excited; it took me some time to digest this blessing.

After my initial excitement, I knew I had to be properly prepared because I wanted to make a good impression. I quickly reined in my excitement and found a trainer to help get me ready to go play in Iceland.

My rigorous schedule saw me training at least five days a week, sometimes six. There was one point at which I had started to push myself too hard in order to be ready. My trainer Trey Hart suggested that I scale back on my training sessions because it was undesirable that I peak too soon. My training sessions consisted of a combination of gym workouts, as well as physical and football training. When I did my first fitness test, I scored 23 on the Nike Spark Test. I trained for approximately six weeks after that first test with my trainer and then I re-did the test. This time I scored 40 which is really good since professional female footballers need to score between 33 and 40 on this type of test to be considered as being at peak fitness level.

The training I did was the hardest training I have ever completed throughout my playing career thus far, because I wanted to be as ready as possible. I ensured that I prepared myself not only physically and mentally, but also emotionally and spiritually. I knew that I would have had to be able to adapt to the people - teammates and coach included, as well as the new environment, food, and culture. But as a woman of substance I was not daunted by this challenge and by the time I left Trinidad, I was confident that I was ready. It's always hard leaving my mother, my family members, and friends behind, but it was to do something I love, and knowing that they believe in me, gave me an extra boost of confidence.

My contract period was from May 1st to September 15th. I had to fortify myself mentally because I knew that Iceland would be terribly cold, but I was ready for the challenge. On the first day I arrived in Iceland I was in awe, the scenery was so beautiful that I fell in love immediately and I was excited to see more. When I met my teammates, they were cool and the coach was super nice as well. I was welcomed with open arms by my teammates, coach, the children I would later coach, and the people in the small town where we resided. To a large extent, I found the citizens of Iceland to be very friendly and polite, and I started to learn more about the culture and how they operate as a first-world country. Learning more about Iceland proved to be interesting indeed. One of the greatest challenges proved to be learning the Icelandic language and many a time I bit my tongue trying to pronounce their words correctly. I was determined though because I wanted to be able to communicate with my teammates and the wonderful people in my new temporary home.

Iceland is a very large place but the population is small. The country has approximately half of a million people living there. The towns are very small. The city, Reykjavik, has the largest concentration of citizens. In the capital, there is more to do than in the small towns. The town where I was staying was Reydarfjordur, and there wasn't much to do there, in terms of cinema, etc, but there was a lot of sightseeing and little adventures that one could go on. It takes eight hours to the capital if commuting by car or forty minutes if travelling by plane.

I would definitely play in Iceland again. The environment was very peaceful, not too busy and I like places like that. However, I did not appreciate the cold weather. Lol. I thoroughly enjoyed the experience I garnered coaching the children, and this fuelled the thoughts that I would like to potentially become a coach one day, once the opportunity presents itself.

I am learning not to put my eggs into one basket, so I am looking into pursuing courses in coaching during my free time. I want to be able to qualify myself now so that I can fall seamlessly into what I hope will be my next chapter when I am finished playing - coaching.

Chapter 13

Iceland - The Scenery, People, and Food

I would like to just talk about the scenery - the environment was so beautiful that every morning on waking up, I would usually look outside at the natural ambience of Iceland to start my day. The mountains looked so lovely from both inside and outside. I admired the scenery each day. I was able to witness the largest waterfall, which was epic. On my off days, my homegirl Victoria and I went to different locations to enjoy the beauty of the country. I even have some very beautiful pictures of me enjoying hiking in the cold and enjoying nature. One time, the higher we went up into the mountains, the colder it became, and you know who put up her hand to turn back, me of course. My hands started to freeze and Victoria and the coach who carried us on the hike started laughing at me. I guess I was living up to my nickname "Baby". Being from Tobago which is a tourist attraction island, as we know, is very beautiful with lovely beaches and other things to do but Iceland was a different experience and I fully embraced that new experience.

As I touched on before, the people in the country are very friendly and welcoming. The neighborhood was very small, which meant that everyone knew when new people entered the area. Thus, it didn't take long for the villagers to notice the three internationals - Victoria Swift, my fellow Trinbagonian friend, a United States player, Julie, and me. Everyone noticed we were new and that we had come to play with Leiknir/Hottur. In the first few days following our arrival, we would get stares from the people in the area because we were new to the town. They asked questions here and there because they had heard that we came to play with the football team in the area. Overall I did not have any issues with the people at all and they were often inside very early, maybe because it's cold or simply because Icelandic people cherish family time, a trait I admire. I am thankful to have made a few great new friends.

Since Victoria and I were from Trinidad and Tobago, we cooked most of our food. The seasoning and ingredients that we would use at home were not the same so we had to make a few substitutions. However, we were still able to season our chicken and make regular dishes without having any problems. The rice was a bit different but it was edible. The basic necessities that we use in Trinidad and Tobago such as flour, sardines, milk, cheese, fruits, vegetables, and butter were sold in the stores, so we didn't have much of a problem with food. We got basic items to cook and that was good enough for us. In the area, there were a few restaurants, but more fast-food places.

The coach and one of our teammates, occasionally, invited us to have meals. I must say the dishes were well done. We were treated to familiar dishes such as chicken alfredo, barbecued chicken, ribs, garlic bread, and an Icelandic soup that tasted delicious. I always looked forward to my coach or the parents of my trainees inviting us over to their homes on Sundays to partake of their sumptuous dishes. There were always so many options laid out on the table and to be honest, I like my stomach, so those were happy days. Lol! We even had homemade desserts that tasted really yummy; ice- cream and cake that were also well prepared. Nevertheless, even though I enjoyed my time spent in Iceland, I must say that there is no place like home. I would definitely recommend it to anyone who likes to travel, since it's one of the best places, providing some of the most memorable experiences I've had thus far.

Chapter 14

Stumbling Blocks in My Career

Injury is a player's worst nightmare. My first major injury came while I attended West Texas A&M University. During my first season playing at West Texas, I suffered a high ankle sprain, which caused a bone bruise, excessive swelling, and other severe issues. It was the worst ankle injury that I have ever gotten and was my first stumbling block. The second stumbling block was knee problems. I had been plagued with knee problems from a tender age, and it only worsened as my career advanced. It grew serious to the point that surgery became necessary.

My right knee was operated on first by Dr. Parker in the state of Texas. He told me six to nine weeks would have been my recovery time, but the process took a lot longer than that. After completing the MRI, there were multiple things that had gone wrong with my knee - loose body knee cap, cartilage missing, and fluid in my knee. It took me an entire year for my knee to feel even seventy-five percent normal again.

Going through the recovery process, there were days I felt like my knee wasn't getting better, and this made me depressed. I did intensive therapy exercise, soaked my knee in the seawater early in the mornings and I did weight training to further strengthen the muscles to support the knee. There were days that it was hard to stay motivated, but regardless of how I felt, I never gave up, I kept pushing. Finally, after six months there were notable improvements and that made me happy. Eight months in, I started to do some running. I started to run with a limp until I got to the point at which the limp no longer existed. It would be an entire year before my knee felt ready for me to play again.

Due to overcompensating on the left knee, because the right knee had been injured, I eventually blew that left knee. Thankfully the left knee wasn't as bad as the right, but it still required surgery. The problem with the left knee was that a small piece of cartilage was missing behind the knee cap. The following year after completing the first surgery, I had my second surgery, this time on the left knee. The surgery on my left knee did not take too long to heal; it took me twelve weeks to recover. I took my time to strengthen the left knee and ensure that both my knees were strong and ready to play again. I played with a brace until I felt comfortable enough not to depend on the brace. The two knee surgeries and the ankle injury proved to be the biggest stumbling blocks in my playing career. It was frustrating that I could not have played football for about two years straight, especially since football is one of the avenues of escape that I utilise to take my mind off of life's issues. Not being able to play made things more difficult for me but I made it through because I never gave up.

Part of me becoming a "woman of substance" was being able to also build patience. Waking up every day and staying dedicated to doing exercises twice a day when some days I felt like I wasn't making any progress, required a lot of patience. This was another time in my life where character building occurred because I was able to learn how to strive through adversities. The Lord knows there were times I wanted to give up but I refused to succumb to those feelings. After my first surgery, I had to stay non-weight bearing for four weeks. As a result, I began to put on weight and that made me feel a bit down. On some days I had to literally talk myself into staying motivated because it wasn't easy.

Even though it was a long journey back to being fit to play, experiencing the process of moving from one stage to another, to eventually being able to play again, really humbled me. It was on the road to recovery that I really learnt that you will always face challenges but it is how you deal with those challenges that defines you as a person.

Sometimes God allows us to go through certain situations to see if we would still trust Him. Battling injuries for three years strengthened me. I learnt to rely on God and I was led to remember that the Lord never gives us more than we can bear. I also came to the realisation that being a woman of substance does not absolve one from enduring life's tests, rather, one is presented with the opportunity to choose how one reacts and deals with those situations, and in doing so, one continues to grow.

If you don't go through trials, how would you grow? As I went through the process of healing from those injuries, I had to trust God, the experts, and the process, embrace uncertainty, and believe that it was going to get better one day. Putting my career on hold for three years while experiencing the fear that my career had ended, was quite difficult. However, God made things easier because I prayed and asked for His blessings of good health and strength throughout this trying time. It was only because of God's grace and mercy that I was able to conquer my fears bit by bit and I am eternally grateful to Him for seeing me through.

Chapter 15

The Positive Impact of Football in My Life

Overall, football has really impacted my life in a positive manner. It has helped me to be disciplined, grow patient and develop mental toughness and good time management skills. It has also helped me to become dedicated to achieving my goals and I have learnt to be more respectful to others. Through football, I was afforded the opportunity to earn my degrees, travel to various countries, and establish many meaningful and long-lasting friendships. Football helped me to understand that if I want anything in life, I would need to have a good work ethic and I would need to work hard towards achieving it. The game taught me to have the right attitude towards whatever I would like to achieve. I became responsible and was able to make good decisions. As my character has developed, it led to me becoming more aggressive towards accomplishing my goals. I became more goal-oriented and level-headed.

Apart from football, I have always been extremely passionate about business. How fortunate was I then, that one of my passions facilitated my fulfillment of the other. It was my football talent that afforded me the scholarship to attend university, where I was able to earn my degree in Business Management. The discipline I learnt through being a footballer would have provided me with sufficient practice to exhibit the discipline that would become necessary for me to fulfil my dream of establishing my own business, and so I was totally prepared for the process.

Thus, whenever the question is posed about my football experience having contributed to my rise as a woman of substance, the answer is always an unequivocal "Yes". The values I have learnt, the experiences I have enjoyed, and the opportunities that I have been afforded as a result of playing football, have definitely contributed to my personal, professional, financial, and spiritual growth, thereby enhancing my status as a woman of substance.

Chapter 16

Fearful of Failure or Lack of Faith?

On the journey of becoming a woman of substance and once you start to get close to God, there would be many tests that would come your way. One of those tests I had to fight against is being fearful. Fear has a way of keeping us in bondage. Fear can put a complete halt to anything you want to achieve, whether it is spiritually, mentally, physically. Once fear gets the better of you, you can feel there is no forward movement. Fear can cause you to become doubtful, afraid to take chances, can lower your self-esteem and so many other negatives can happen.

At no time should you allow fear to take over your mind, hence the reason you have to have faith and break that cycle by praying and asking God to help you to stop being fearful and for you to develop an attitude of faith. God never gave us a spirit of fear, so as a woman of substance you have to develop the attitude to be bold and courageous. As we know, Rome wasn't built in a day, one of my favorite sayings is, "a journey of a million miles starts with one step". One of the things that fuels a woman of substance, is being able to have strong faith. Don't fall victim to fear, you would never be able to accomplish anything if you do not have faith and believe in your capability to achieve what you want.

Along my journey of becoming a woman of substance, I have some phrases I use to motivate myself. One of those motivational phrases, I tell myself is "faith over fear". That is one of the phrases I often use to push myself. That doesn't have to be your phrase, but these are some of the strategies you can use to motivate yourself whenever fear tries to step in. Don't give up, push through fear. Yes, changes aren't always easy, it all would take time, but once you have faith, fear has no dominion over you. Always remember that throughout your life. Note that becoming a woman of substance is a process. You cannot feel like you can wake up one day and say I am a woman of substance. Each day you have to take a leap of faith and tell yourself you can. The word "can't" should not be in your vocabulary at any point. Being a woman of substance, you have to know that you would be a constant work in progress. You never stop learning!

Throughout my life, I had moments where fear stepped into my life and I had to find a way to overcome it. First, I changed my mindset towards what I was facing. I tried to reframe negative thoughts and adopt more positive thoughts. By adopting positive thoughts, I realized my faith gradually increased, especially as I prayed and asked God to help me by removing fear from my life and replacing it with faith. Change starts with you! I am a strong believer that prayer changes people and things, and that was one of the major factors that helped me to deal with fear better. The Lord worked in me and removed the spirit of fear. I had first-hand experience of how to put God first in my life allowed other aspects of my life to improve. I became more ambitious and confident, and my self-esteem improved. My overall outlook became a positive one. I believe that once God is at the pinnacle of your life, you can conquer anything in life. I have since developed an attitude that will not allow anything to deter me or cause me to be fearful. If I want to achieve something, I am willing to do what it takes to achieve any goal.

Fear can really hinder progress. It can force you to stay stagnant. My story is a living testimony, of someone who didn't allow fear to deprive her of happiness. When I replaced fear with faith, I became unstoppable. One quote I often use a lot from the Bible is, "Seek ye first the kingdom of God and all things shall be added unto you" (Matthew 6:33). I like this quote because too many times we lack faith and focus on the things we have no control over, instead of focusing on what we can control over and let God do His part. Faith without works is dead. We also need to remember that the Lord knows us best, so we need to really focus on him and let him lead and direct our path.

Chapter 17

More Women Becoming Successful in Sports and Globally

Though there are many issues surrounding women in sports, I believe that things have been gradually improving. Some of the issues facing women in sports include inequality of pay, lack of funding, and other related factors. This is not an issue in only a few countries but globally. The female aspects of most sports tend to be struggling in some way or the other. Since I am into football, I was able to gain first-hand experience with paygrade issues and gender inequality. One perfect example is the United States national women's soccer team which filed a lawsuit against its federation for being underpaid in comparison to the men's national team. The United States women's national team has won the World Cup many times, even securing back-to-back titles The men's team, on the other hand, hasn't come close to winning, yet they earn more money than the women. This scenario is proof that not only are women fully capable of achieving great feats, but they are capable of doing so in the face of adversity. It is my belief that struggling through and overcoming issues, especially where it concerns issues of inequality between men and women, is a great contributor to the building of our character and much of what helps us blossom into "women of substance".

Creating and focusing on positives as a "woman of substance" really helps build strong women in society. One thing I know is that we women are stronger than we think, we just have to tap into the strength that exists within us all. I know that it is easier said than done but we have to push. Living in what is popularly deemed "a man's world" isn't easy and it's not that women should compete with men, but we can adopt the positive qualities that some possess of being success-driven, empowered, and relentless about achieving their goals. Many times as women, the reality is that we may have to work a bit harder to accomplish our goals and/or to receive the recognition that we deserve, however, this simply lends itself to cementing our status as women of substance, because as the popular saying goes, "Pressure creates diamonds; fire refines gold".

Globally, women are becoming more successful today, and they are exploring more opportunities which is great. Research has shown that women are dominating and

WOMAN OF SUBSTANCE

achieving more in this new era of the twenty-first century. More women are becoming "women of substance" juggling motherhood, marriage, full-time careers and are still pursuing their goals. History boasts of several women who may be lauded as women of substance because of their roles in women's suffrage activism and securing some of the rights that women currently enjoy. Women like Eleanor Roosevelt, Elizabeth Cady, and Rosa Parks to name a few became ideal images of women of substance as they demonstrated class, dignity, humility, and quiet strength, as they stood firm in their beliefs of what is right and worked tirelessly and steadfastly to pave a smoother pathway for subsequent generations of women. I am thankful that I would have opened my mind to learning about these influential women in my college History class because I really believe that one of the traits of a true woman of substance, is being open to garnering new knowledge and readjusting one's thinking as this new information is assimilated.

Women of substance are now becoming pastors, prime ministers, presidents, engineers, business owners, etc. They are now earning degrees and doctorates and ingratiating themselves in places where they can have more reach and therefore make a meaningful difference in their communities, countries, and the world at large. In my birthplace of Trinidad and Tobago, we have had both our first female prime minister and the first female president take office within the last eleven years, and we have seen this become a growing trend regionally and internationally as well. Again, this chapter was not penned with the intention of pitting the accomplishments of women against those of men, but merely to highlight females who have been making strides, dominating and breaking barriers, and removing stereotypes of things that were previously established and accepted.

Of course, I'm sure you know that these women of substance did not just wake up and have these things just happen for them. They would have identified areas in which they felt a change was needed and in which they felt a burning desire to bring about change, they would have made plans about how they intended to achieve their set goals, and they would have taken the action necessary to ensure that they ended up in positions to affect change. These women of substance would have made many sacrifices and trodden on even in the difficult moments, to ensure that their goals were realised. They made sacrifices, set goals and they did not stop until they achieved those goals.

Woman of substance, what is preventing you from being unstoppable? The only person who should be able to possess such power is you. Get out of your own way and start making strides towards fulfilling your true potential.

Chapter 18

Fellow Woman of Substance, Do Not Settle

As the previous chapter mentioned, more women are becoming successful globally and I believe that cycle could go on if we as women understand that the power is in our hands. The decision is yours and how badly you want success. This book is a powerful guide for inspiring young women not to settle, but to utilise the resources that are available to enable them to become great. Be relentless! Be courageous! Be fearless! Be resilient! No matter what the world throws at you, keep the same energy. The Lord has given each of us the ability to do great things, do not limit yourself. Do not let what's going on in the world distract you from doing what you want to do. Focus on the things you have control over and leave God to take care of the things that are out of your control.

The secret to finding your strength is through prayer. It works! God is real! I am a strong advocate of PUSHing - Praying Until Something Happens. It's imperative that you build a relationship with God, you will experience myriad benefits. Through prayer, God helps you to see things more clearly. Fasting and praying work tremendously. God is a forgiving God; he hears you once you repent and fully commit yourself to Him. As you would have read in previous chapters, I have encountered my share of challenges in life, even seeing myself get to the point of what I thought was no return. But God! Jesus found me at my weakest and showed me the light and gave me His strength. God sees and knows all of our struggles, we simply have to learn to trust in Him. God is the only one that can help us find our true happiness, we just have to have faith and allow Him to do what He does best, which is work. You are also required to be patient, trusting that His timing is perfect, He is never late. As your relationship with God deepens, your life would gradually change. Trust me when I say that all of your struggles would not have been in vain. All the blessings coming your way will be entirely worth the wait.

As my evolution as a woman of substance continues, I have been training myself not to settle for a mediocre living but to aim for the beyond unexpected limits. It is important to note that the phrase "mediocre living" has nothing to do with financial wealth and everything to do with my self-development. In my current thought process, I consider the goals I am desirous of achieving, how badly I want change, what is required to get to where I want to be, and what I am willing to forfeit in the pursuit of my passions and my purpose. I have prepared myself to accept that failures will come, but I have also committed to rise and keep going when they do. I have pledged to do all the work that I can and to let God do the rest. Above all, I have decided to enjoy the journey; too often we are focused on the finish line and we forget to enjoy the journey. When I recount to my children and grandchildren, the story of my journey, I must be able to do so quoting the words of Michael Jordan, "I failed over and over and that's why I was successful".

Chapter 19

Personal Life

This chapter was very difficult for me to write because admittedly I do not like to talk about my personal life. However, since I want my story to inspire others, I am aware that I cannot only highlight the good aspects of my life, so here goes...

I have always been a family-oriented person, dreaming of having a husband and one or two children, a home big enough to comfortably accommodate my family, and a contented life. Growing up, the word boyfriend held no meaning apart from referring to a boy whom I considered to be a friend. When my friends would boast of having boyfriends, I would say that I also had one in an effort to fit in. It was only when I got a bit older, that I entered into a serious relationship, where the word "boyfriend" had a bit more meaning. I was 17 years old when that relationship began and having lasted for over five years, it was and is, the only long-term, serious relationship in which I've been.

As we know, many relationships are often nice at first, then as the honeymoon phase fades and the fog of euphoria clears, your partner's true colors come more sharply into focus. After a while the problems came, gradually stifling my happiness and sending me into a tailspin of depression, shame, low self-esteem, unhealthy weight loss, and despair. I was ashamed to discuss what I was experiencing with my friends and loved ones and when I did mention anything, it was never the entire story, just surface details. I was inexperienced and ill-equipped to handle the problems in my relationship and chose not to seek advice from external sources. The effects of the relationship were taking a brutal toll on me and I felt like I had lost myself.

I saw many signs that should have prompted me to end the relationship, but I am a person who thinks that people deserve to be given chances to correct their behaviour, after all, if not for God's patience with, the forgiveness of and mercy and grace towards us, where would we be? Unfortunately, harbouring that situation for longer than I should have, caused me more pain. My partner knew that at age seventeen I did not have much experience with relationships and he took full advantage of the situation and my feelings for him. The relationship drained me mentally, emotionally, physically, and spiritually. I spent many nights crying. For a very long time, I had lost my smile and if I did smile, it was forced and fake. I loathed showing weakness so I often kept a big smile on my face to maintain the facade that all was well. Inside I felt like I was always angry and when I was too emotionally exhausted to fake smiles, I found myself snapping at every little thing that anyone told me. I saw myself hit rock bottom. However, the good thing about being at rock bottom is that the only place to go from there is up.

My journey to recovery began when I really started to pour my heart out to God, asking Him to help me through this situation. I have always been passionate about God, but I became even more so after God met me at my weakest and led me to find myself again. I would question the Lord about why I was going through this bad breakup and how such a nice person like me could get messed over so badly. It was then that it dawned on me that we often make decisions that lead to our own heartaches and then we question God, but in actuality, we had not sought His guidance in the first place.

Though that was a stage of my life which brought me much shame, guilt, and pain, I was confident that God would rescue me, and I am thankful that He did. I spent countless nights asking God for His strength to overcome this situation and even though I was experiencing that trying time, I never lost faith. One of the things I prayed fervently for was being able to see happier days. I yearned to be able to smile genuinely again and to laugh and talk without feeling the pain of what I had been experiencing.

My breakthrough came as a result of my trusting God and constantly praying. My life further improved when I got baptized and started surrounding myself with more positive people. I was in college when I was on the road to recovery from this relationship and there was a counselling department on campus, so I made the decision to speak with a counsellor. She was an African American lady and I felt safe opening up to her because she did not know me and she genuinely wanted to help me to beat that struggle I had been facing. In addition to prayer, frequenting positive environments, and fraternising with those with positive outlooks, counselling played a pivotal role in changing my mindset and ensuring my healing.

At first, I regretted that relationship and I hastily decided that relationships were not for me. As I continued to heal and things got better, I accepted that my then partner had not been the best person for me. I decided that I would not change anything about the way things had progressed in the relationship and that instead of dwelling on the negatives, I would focus on the positives that could be extracted from that situation.

I now see that that bad relationship played a critical part in shaping me into a woman of substance. It caused me to build a tremendous amount of strength and made me into a more spiritually grounded person. I started to think very differently about relationships. I became wiser and more meticulous about my choices. My eyes opened to the fact that I deserve good things and I grew less inclined to settle for less. My energy grew and my belief system strengthened. I set the standards for what I would be willing to accept in relationships henceforth. I decided that in the future I would attempt to gain insight into a man's way of thinking, his character, beliefs, and intentions before opting to pursue a relationship. I realized that patience is the key not only towards establishing relationships but in life in general. I learnt that seeking the Lord's guidance to help me to make better choices, is of paramount importance. The next man with whom I involve myself must be approved by God and I just feel in my spirit that our relationship is God-ordained. Now I can say that I understand life from a different perspective. We all have been through something in life, we all are affected differently but there is always light at the end of the tunnel.

Experience has been by far my greatest teacher. I would admit to being very guarded with my heart now and I am very skeptical about whom I allow into my life because I am not about to make the same mistake twice. Currently, I am single by choice, patiently awaiting the man I know God has for me. I am not prepared to enter into another relationship that would steal my peace and cause me to forget the woman of substance whom I have become. Everyone deserves to be loved, and I am desirous of being loved. However, I strongly affirm that love should be offered with respect and a high level of communication.

In these times of social media facilitating society's need to present false representations of reality, offer unsolicited opinions on the ways in which others choose to live, and influence the lives of others, I find it important not to be misled and to stick to one's ideals. The content posted on social media has a way of making one feel as though they are missing out or falling behind on what they ought to be achieving at particular stages in their lives. Please know that your life is not scripted by man, but is controlled by God.

Remember that one of the key criteria of being a woman of substance is being able to choose wisely. Be patient in waiting for what you know you deserve and refrain from making snap decisions that could be detrimental, all in the name of trying to create an image. Create your own image of what love and a happy and functional relationship look like to you and do not sell yourself short. Make it difficult for a man to walk into your life and disrupt your peace. If that man really cares for you, he would understand that you are a woman of substance and would aspire to maintain and enhance your quality as such.

Know that you possess the power to set the tone for how you wish to be treated.

During this phase of my life, I have opted to remain celibate and save myself for marriage. It's a personal path that I have decided to trod because I believe that it is in keeping with my desire to deepen my relationship with God and have Him be the centre of my life, and it is the right choice for me. I know and respect that as individuals we all have the right to decide what's right for us and I am in no way critical of anyone who chooses differently. I am simply sharing the way I decide to move forward and what has been working for me. I believe that a huge part of the way our lives progress is dependent upon the choices we make and that whatever choices we make can either affect us positively or negatively. Your ball is in your court, you have to know the life you really want and take the relevant steps to affect the changes that you desire.

I have decided that I would like someone with whom I am equally yoked so that even while focusing on the relationship, my focus on God would be shared, supported, and strengthened. I am taking my time with my next relationship because I don't just want a boyfriend, I am preparing myself for marriage, and to be someone's wife. I'd rather be patient and make a good choice than rush and be miserable where more harm than good is the result. I am using this time of being single to focus on my spiritual life, on being financially stable, emotionally prepared, and mentally ready to be able to sustain my family and provide in the way I may need to when that time comes. Moreover, I'm concentrating on loving myself because this is the basis of making correct decisions for oneself and for being able to love another person as they deserve.

I understand that things are not always black and white and plans don't always go as expected. However, I see no harm in knowing what I want and preparing for it. Though single, I am open to meeting and interacting with new people, but I am only willing to commit to someone who makes sense to my life. The ordeal I endured during my relationship taught me to observe, to consult with those who love me and whose opinions I value because of their knowledge and experience, and their ability to have a clearer perspective, and most importantly, to wait for God's direction before making a decision.

Chapter 20

My Driving Force

As the previous chapter intimated, there was a point in my life when I had hit rock bottom. I was depressed, I felt broken inside, and my self-esteem was low. I felt like something was missing from my life and, I just couldn't figure out at first, what it was. Throughout that trying time in my life though I could not think clearly, one thing I never stopped doing, was praying. As I continued to pray, gradually I started to see improvements in my life. Thus, who would I say is the driving force of my life - JESUS! The Lord picked me up when I was down and He showed me mercy. As I developed a relationship with Him and continued praying, I eventually started to witness depression, hate, strife, sadness, hurt, negativity, the spirit of fear, slink away from my life.

I took my spiritual life to another level by accepting Jesus Christ as my Lord and my Savior. It brought great joy to my soul; it was one of the best feelings. God has had a huge influence on my life, personally molding and shaping the woman of substance that I am today. I think the challenging times that I encountered, were God's way of emptying me, allowing me to discard my former self so that He could fill me up, strengthen me and make me whole in Him.

I can state with confidence that without God's guidance, I would not have been where I am today. I know that my life is a living testimony because I am no longer where I used to be. I am not perfect but I have grown, and I try to be a better person each day. I have developed an attitude that no matter what happens, I am not going to allow anything to get in the way of my happiness or in the way of me praising God for His unfailing love and mercy.

After going through these different stages and realizing how important it is to put God at the top of my life, I decided to get baptized on January 26th, 2014. The church was Konania Christian Fellowship in Dallas, Texas. Since making this lifelong commitment to God, I have seen my life improve by leaps and bounds. I became more spiritual, more confident, bolder in making decisions, stronger, wiser, and more empowered. I have seen my self-esteem improve and I am now a positive thinker. I am learning to trust and depend on God in everything. Little by little, God has been grooming me and fashioning me into the "woman of substance" He created me to be.

After what I had experienced, it was only after placing God first that I was able to find true happiness. I can testify that true happiness comes from putting God first in your life and allowing his Holy Spirit to lead and direct your path. Life is a journey and while on that journey, you would have many obstacles; God is the One who will ensure that you evade or surmount every one of them. I will admit to occasionally falling short, but that would not deter me from trying to do the right things.

I will never stop promoting Jesus, He is my rock. Since I know that Rome wasn't built in a day, I ask God for patience because I know His timing is perfect. If there's one thing that I have learnt, is that we need to stop blaming God for the negative occurrences in our lives. Instead, we should grasp the opportunity to show God our weakness so that He could show us His strength. It's not too late to change your life. Change comes from within, God has worked on my life and He is able and willing to work on yours.

Chapter 21

My Second Motivator

I say that she is my second motivator because it is with a reverence that I always recognise God's precedence in my life as the Source from which all good things in my life originate. Thus, my second motivator is none other than my mother.

My mother worked as a waitress at the Turtle Beach Rex Hotel. Despite working very hard, she earned a small salary, yet she always found a way to ensure that my sisters and I had the necessities, especially those that would eventually lead to us experiencing a better life. I have seen her struggle to make ends meet, doing what was necessary to make sure that food remained on our table. Ensuring that my sisters and I obtained an education was of paramount importance to my mother, so in spite of how limited her resources were, she ensured that we were always provided with our uniforms, books, and tools, and money to attend school.

At times when the money wasn't sufficient, my mother did extra jobs to ensure that we had the necessities. I specifically recall my mother resorting to selling cigarettes and paper to earn extra money to send us to school. Though I knew that it could not have been easy being a single mother of four children, I really hated that she had to engage in this particular activity. However, due to the large number of people in my village who engaged in smoking cannabis in those days, selling cigarettes and paper proved to be a lucrative business, often providing additional revenue to enable my siblings and me to attend school. That did not make me feel any better about it, because at that time I was becoming more serious about my walk with God. There were occasions when I would have been home alone and people came to make a purchase, I would be hesitant and at times I even hid, just to avoid engaging in what I considered to be a nefarious activity. Looking back I realise that my mother was simply demonstrating a trait of any true woman of substance - the willingness to do what is necessary, once it is within the parameters of the law, to provide for her children and lay the foundation for them to experience a better life than she has had.

It would be years later until my mother received her breakthrough, first securing a better job and then opening her own vegetable store, where she was able to make money to live a bit more comfortably. Once again I saw my woman as being a woman of substance because even when things were difficult, my mother did not throw her hands in the air and call it quits. She continued to work diligently and strive toward and stay prepared for embracing better when it came her way. It is from my mother that I would have inherited my drive, resilience, and commitment to working hard to achieve what I desire.

My motivation to succeed came mainly from seeing my mother struggle. Her selfless sacrifices motivated me to excel academically and athletically; the thought of allowing all of her hard work to go to waste just did not sit well with me. It was my mother's commitment to making sure that I excelled academically, that propelled me to attend college abroad. I felt that attending a college abroad would have enabled me to either earn a degree that would get me a good job or gain enough exposure during my stint at college to secure a professional contract. It was also she who inspired me to work towards becoming an entrepreneur. My mission has always been that in spite of what career path I had chosen after completing my degree, it had to provide me with the capability to financially sustain my mother and my sisters.

Observing all that my mother did to provide for her family, at times caused me much pain and now I am eager to do whatever I can to repay her for all of her hard work. She can get anything from me and as long as I am able, I will spoil her. I want to provide her with everything she would need or want because she deserves the best and more. Always a very hardworking, kind, sweet, genuine, and strong woman, I love my mother dearly and I would do anything to ensure that she is happy. I only have one mother and I intend to cherish her all the days of my life.

I applaud my mother for her diligence in her duty as a parent, because she provided for us even though resources were limited. She was not always able to give everything I wanted, but she certainly provided everything that I needed, and this experience humbled me. Additionally, my mother's aim to not just provide for us financially and materialistically, but to expose my sisters and me to opportunities that she never had as a child, fuelled my desire to make her proud.

I can safely say that my first interaction with a true "woman of substance" came from being nurtured by a mother whose parenting skills, work ethic, and general deportment have always been beyond reproach. One of the qualities of my mother that I find most admirable is her perseverance. Never one to be daunted or have her efforts thwarted by a problem, she always finds a way to move the mountains in her path. Thankfully, I adopted that same mentality from a tender age.

Woman of Substance

To my mind, a woman of substance is one who knows that she may not have been able to enjoy her present accomplishments without the significant and unselfish contribution of others, and who continues to acknowledge and demonstrate her gratitude for the same. Thank you, Mommy, for the invaluable impact you have had on my becoming a woman of substance.

Chapter 22

My Third Motivator

My third motivator is definitely a combination of Burt Stuart and my immediate family. Burt played a great part in my life - he guided me like a father and he helped me in numerous ways. He was always a great source of motivation and he never gave up on me. Burt ensured that I was equipped with all that was necessary for me to succeed. That included paying for extra school lessons, providing financial support, and being a source of spiritual support. Since he so effectively fulfilled the role of a father in my life, he helped take the strain off my mother who was a single parent with four children, and for this, I am eternally grateful. I cannot thank God enough for blessing my life with Burt's presence.

Through the role he so willingly adopted and played in my life, Burt taught me about being a person of substance. After all, the substance is not gender-specific but is dependent upon the characteristics that an individual possesses. Not many men are capable of loving and nurturing children they did not father, but Burt did just that, and in doing so, he taught me that the true substance of an individual is rooted in the beauty of his heart, and blossoms through his character.

Both Burt and my family members have always been there for me and words can never adequately express how much I appreciate having them accompany me on this journey that is my life. They have always supported me every step of the way. No matter what issues I may face, I always have my family and Burt to turn to. They have motivated me and have remained my rock-solid support system.

My family's assistance has been much more than financial; they have supported me spiritually, emotionally, physically, and mentally. Their influence in my life has helped to hone the depth of personality and character which makes it fitting for me to be viewed as a woman of substance. I am grateful to them all and continue to aim to make them proud.

Chapter 23

Society's Ability to Affect Our Thinking and Our Lives

Society can have a positive effect on our lives or a negative effect, depending on the choices that we make. Racism, injustice, prejudice, poverty, social media influence, hate, strife, and other factors can all negatively impact our lives. How can we trump these situations or rebound from these types of issues? We must first change our minds. There are situations over which we have control and those we simply cannot control. As such, in order to free our minds, we need to focus on the things that fall within our sphere of control. If we want to progress and to live in peace, we have to stop allowing society to dictate our actions. There are certain things in our lives that will come to pass and threaten the good habits and patterns of positive thinking that we have tried to cultivate. However, it is how we react in these situations that would determine how easily we are able to move on and ultimately our happiness. Do not fall victim to societal norms of spewing hatred, instead, rise above hate and show love. Don't allow what may be happening in this world, cause you to be negative. Remember that love conquers all.

Change starts from within ourselves. As I always say, be the change you would like to see in the world. We need to rise up and be our brother's keeper. If each of us changes our mindset and makes a conscious decision and takes decisive steps toward living in love, the world can be a better place. We also need to understand that we are all humans, we are not perfect. But if we are, to be honest with ourselves, we would see that we can all be better in some way. We all have choices whether it is to be bitter or to choose love. Peace is there for everyone; we just have to believe and make that our choice. The more we live in peace the happier we are throughout life.

On my journey to becoming a woman of substance, I discovered that I had to fight through different situations, but I always knew there would have been light at the end of the tunnel. We have to keep a positive attitude regardless of what we may be facing. Life is to be lived to the fullest. Remember the aim is to do the things that would make us happy, adjust ourselves when undesirable situations occur, and no matter what, never stop, always keep moving. There is a time for everything. Love unconditionally, we need a society saturated with love and filled with better people. Take the time to contribute to, see and appreciate the good in everything.

Chapter 24

Leaders Who Have Inspired Me

Without a shadow of a doubt, I would always put God at the top of the list of leaders who inspire me. After all, God is the reason why I am alive. The more I commit myself to God, the more I see myself become happier. I read my Bible regularly and by doing that, I have become more spiritually inclined. God motivates me to live a clean life. With the strength of God, I value living a better life each day and push towards achieving my goals. The Lord has helped me to fight many battles which I have been able to conquer. As a believer, I know that the Lord endured a lot of pain on the cross. I take the liberty of saying that what we are is God's gift to us, but what we become is our gift to God. He has shown me the true definition of a real leader and He inspires me to be a better person each day. I can go on all day about the Lord's goodness and mercies. I just thank God for knowledge, because without His foundation in me I would not have become the person I am today. On my journey of developing a relationship with God, I was able to build inner strength that I never thought I possessed. I have placed the Lord at the center of my life, and come what may, that is where He will remain. Without the Lord, I would not be the confident, intelligent, caring, loving, ambitious person I am today. Each day, I am thankful that I am able to blossom into a stronger individual because of the Lord's grace.

Another source of inspiration was found in the person of Maya Angelou. As an avid fan of women empowerment initiatives, I admired her for her relentless effort as a woman who was willing to succeed at anything she tried to accomplish. Having been an author and prolific poet, she really impacted people's lives in a positive manner, including mine. Maya Angelou was a very influential figure and many persons worldwide respected her for all her efforts, her empowering leadership, and her legacy lives on today. One of her quotes which has become my favourite is, "You have encountered many defeats but you must not be defeated". I must say that as the quote alludes, I have been through some difficult days, but on those days when I felt defeated, this particular quote of Maya Angelou, really inspired me to keep going, as I told myself I must not be defeated.

Maya Angelou's accomplishments and her drive have caused a change in many lives. Based on information gathered through personal research, I learnt that besides being a brilliant author, Maya Angelou was one of the women who fought for civil rights alongside other notable women like Susan B Anthony, Rosa Parks, and Sojourner Truth. These women were among the first to put in the hard work to surmount the difficulties faced by women in earlier days and help us to gain the freedom and privileges that we currently enjoy. Understanding the history of what these women endured not only inspired me but has led to me appreciating life a bit more.

I applaud these women for their great efforts to help women like myself feel empowered and to be proactive about accomplishing goals that are ordinarily beyond the expectations of what a woman can achieve. It's a great joy to see that women are becoming more successful today. We have to choose our path in life. Maya Angelou and these other women have encouraged me to create my own legacy by not keeping knowledge to myself but sharing it in the hope of inspiring others. I had never envisioned that I would be writing a book or earning degrees because I did not like school, but here I am, in possession of a changed outlook and continuously striving to become a better person. If I can do it, I believe that you can too!!!

My desires and accomplishments don't have to be yours, but it is important that you have goals; there must be something that you like doing, have a talent for, or want to do. Take a chance and chase your dreams. I know that I am in no way a perfect person, but I will never allow that to stop me from trying to influence positive changes by inspiring people in any way that I can. My hope is that by using this book to share my story others would read it and feel compelled to start their journeys toward enjoying their own successes and creating their own legacies. Over the years, I have learnt that to have a positive influence on someone's life, is a blessing, not just to the person being influenced, but the influencer as well. To be a blessing to someone would bring me immense joy because I view it as my opportunity to serve others, I see it as giving thanks for all of those people who have positively impacted my life and I strongly believe that there are many people who just need to know that once there is life, hope exists.

Other people who have inspired me are Nelson Mandela and Devon Franklin. Like Maya Angelou, Nelson Mandela is a world-renowned individual. By his very existence and the amazing level of resilience demonstrated by him, especially during his twenty-seven-year incarceration, Nelson Mandela has proven to be a role model to many, helping them to remain resolute in their beliefs, to fight for what is right, and to maintain courage in the face of even the greatest adversity. I find him inspirational particularly because I have a burning desire to affect the changes I want to see in the world. Nelson

Mandela's work ethic, drive, sacrifices, and passion are really impressive. One of his quotes that I like very much is "Education is the most powerful weapon which you can use to change the world". I find this to be deep because I strongly believe that education exposes us to the necessary knowledge that we can use to affect change. As one of my other favorite authors opined, "Money doesn't make you rich, knowledge does". You should never stop learning; you should always keep an open mind to learning new things. Throughout his life, Nelson Mandela equipped himself to fight for what he felt was right by using every opportunity presented to him to educate himself and become very knowledgeable, and so I feel encouraged to keep reading and educating myself. My reading on Nelson Mandela's life, struggles, and achievements revealed that he showed bravery, and tenacity on his life's journey. I applaud him for his tireless efforts and I am grateful for the ways in which he would have impacted my life.

I recall reading Devon Franklin's book, "The Wait" and enjoying his story of how he has been able to be successful thus far. The book centered around his having been celibate, described how he met his wife and outlined the steps they took to maintain their discipline in refraining from engaging in pre-marital sex. The book served to provide both information and encouragement since I am currently practising celibacy. Devon Franklin is also a Pastor; I listen to his sermons and he always leaves a lasting impression on me when he preaches. I am a strong believer in God, and since he is a believer as well, his passion and hunger for God inspire me. Pastor Franklin juggles spending time with his wife, writing books, preaching, working out, and other projects, and I like the fact that he leads a balanced life. I believe that it speaks of his ability to be very organized and that reminds me of myself.

I was privy to one of Devon Franklin's quotes which says, "Don't downgrade your dream to match your reality. upgrade your faith to match your destiny". I like this quote because I am a young, aspiring person who is hungry for success. I am using my faith as a tool to fuel my drive to fulfill my destiny. Pastor Franklin continues to bring about change in the lives of others, through his preaching, his beliefs, and his lifestyle, and I find that to be quite admirable. Like him, I want to share my story with others and have my life be a testimony that would encourage others to conquer their fears, live by faith, and be courageous enough to stick to their ideals.

Not every person who I have viewed as a role model has been as widely known as Maya Angelou or Devon Franklin. Take for example Cali Llyod who is a soccer player. Having been the United States national soccer team Captain for several years, she has won many major competitions such as the World Cup and other invitational tournaments. Llyod is a really good leader and an exceptional player. I was privileged to play against Cali when Trinidad and Tobago played against the United States senior women's team. I admired her hard-working mentality, her unique leadership qualities, and her hunger to be the best not only at football, at everything she undertook. Cali operates very professionally, being very serious about being the best at what she does, and during her career, she has scored an impressive number of goals both for the United States and for her professional clubs. Cali's commitment to succeed, her hard-working effort, her dedication, her humility which drives her to become successful, and her motivation on and off the field, are very inspiring and remind me of myself. I laud her competitive spirit, her tendency to be resilient, and her commitment to always leading her team well as the captain.

Cali often speaks words of wisdom and one of her sayings that remains with me is, "Motivation is a fire from within. No one can hand it to you. But no one can take it away either". Cali is driven by intrinsic motivation and self-confidence and this accounts for her fantastic performance on the field and her success off the field. Over time I have adopted the same mindset, motivating myself to create my own path and pushing to achieve my goals. Thus far, I have been doing really well, but there is always room for improvement. I am very optimistic and open to what life has to offer to me. I consider Cali to be a great role model and I have no problem emulating her as I push towards achieving my own goals. I believe as you let your light shine, you unconsciously give others permission to do the same. Let's spread more positivity with those whom we encounter. If each of us tries to be positive, we can make the world a better place. My aim is to keep pushing to become the best version of myself and to be a positive voice to others.

As previously stated, I have played for the Trinidad and Tobago National Women's team for over ten years and so Maylee has been my captain for a very long time. Maylee is the type of leader who is very bold, courageous, hardworking, outgoing, fearless, and empowered. She is a no-nonsense and very outspoken person and her attitude to win is amazing. Whether she is injured or not she leads by example. Maylee's fighting spirit never wanes. I like that about her because she has a lot of heart. Her style may not appeal to many, but many respect her, and I believe this to be extremely important. As a leader, you must be able to do what it takes to ensure that you are eliciting the desired behaviour and performance from your followers. Maylee leads by example and her players have no choice but to fall in line. She often puts the needs of others ahead of hers, which I believe is a trait of any good leader.

As a young woman aspiring to be an effective leader, I am taking notes from all these persons that I have mentioned, because they have done many noteworthy things. Each person I have mentioned has opened up my eyes and increased my knowledge. Seeking guidance from people whose ideals I admire, may very well be my first decisive step towards becoming a competent leader because I believe that a leader is always willing to be a lifelong learner and recognises the merit of being teachable. I affirm that sometimes you have to learn to be a good follower before you can become a competent leader.

Chapter 25

Leaders – Are They Born or Made?

An entire chapter of my book has been dedicated to the people whom I consider to be "leaders" and who have inspired me. In that chapter, I would have highlighted God as being the paramount leader, the chief source of inspiration, and my EVERYTHING. Somehow, I believe that many would accept my stance because well, it's God. It is safe to accept His ability to lead with questioning. But what about human beings whom we consider to be leaders? Have you ever pondered upon the frequently asked question about whether leaders are born or made?

Perhaps prior to attempting to answer this question, one needs to have a proper understanding of the concept of leadership. On the journey to becoming a "woman of substance", you would most likely develop leadership skills that would help prepare you to lead. It is important to understand that leadership does not only refer to leading a congregation, organization, or any other particular formal setup; anyone can lead! Leadership is evident in the running of households, in sports where teams are led by captains, in owning your own business, and in leading our child or children in the right way. Get the concept out of your head that you have to be someone highly recognised in society in order to lead. Thus, I am redirected to my earlier question, "Are leaders born or made?"

With the knowledge, that mine is not the only viewpoint that exists, and in an effort to hear diverse opinions, I conducted a mini virtual survey on my social media platforms with my followers, asking them to respond to the aforementioned question. With those results in hand, I discovered that eighty-five percent of my followers felt that leaders are made and fifteen percent of them felt that leaders are born. I spoke to an additional four people who are my close friends, and they too opined that leaders are made. Two people stated that leaders could be both born and made and I felt that they may have had a valid point. One of them further explained that he thought that it was definitely a combination of both because he believed that some people are born with particular personality traits that lead to making them better leaders than others, but unless these qualities are fine-tuned, those gifts or abilities will be wasted. I couldn't help but note that it's the same with sport, as

"Talent without hard work is nothing". No answer is wrong, but some information can cause you to view situations differently. Another commenter reasoned that "You cannot watch a baby in pampers and say he or she is going to be a leader". Lol! If you really consider this statement, it makes sense. In the end, I concluded that this particular question can elicit multiple responses highlighting varying thoughts, opinions, and arguments. Though the question was posed with the aim of hearing others' thoughts and showing how leadership can be viewed in numerous ways, the ultimate goal was to identify ways and means of using leadership traits and skills to advance the aim of becoming a woman of substance.

I didn't think I would have been anyone's role model or anyone's leader, but as I trusted the process and grew into a woman of substance, I became empowered. Before I learnt to lead, I had to learn how to follow. Based on the question of whether leaders are born or made, I would have to say that they are both born and made. But if I had to choose one, I would definitely say that leaders are made. Why? Well, when I was growing up my nickname was "baby" and I lived up to the name. Lol! As I educated myself and gained knowledge not only academically, but generally, and as I matured over the years, I realized that I have what it takes to push myself further.

I then took on the challenge to start doing things that were previously outside of my comfort zone. I began with orchestrating my tournaments, and when it arose, I grasped the opportunity to captain the national team, and in doing so I became a role model to others. When called upon to be a motivational speaker for Metal Industries Company (MIC). I attended leadership seminars and availed myself of the information they offered and I researched other leaders who I thought were inspiring. The aim was to learn about leadership, such that I would be well equipped to be an effective leader and to teach others about leadership.

I can safely say that the leadership traits and skills that I have developed, further fuelled my drive to achieve my goals and helped propel me into becoming a woman of substance. In the past, when I pictured my future self, it was never the image of the person I am today, simply because for as long as I can remember I have always been an introvert, shy, and very sheltered. It took a leap of faith for me to step out into becoming the true self I was ordained to be. I am truly liking the transitions and I recognise that I am a work in progress, a masterpiece in the making. I don't think that I adhere to a specific leadership style; rather, I believe that I incorporate a bit of most of them into how I choose to lead. I find that a combination of charisma and the democratic and transformational leadership styles work best for me.

As I gaze into my future, I do think that I have a lot to offer to inspire others positively. I realize that God has worked on my life in so many ways and I want to use my experiences and knowledge to help motivate others. There are so many ideas swirling in my head about how I can help others to see the good within themselves and to help influence them to accomplish their goals. I know that there are some people who are prompted to do something when they see that others have done it and become successful. I would like to be the reason why someone did not give up on his dreams. It is my aim to continue being a good example to those who look up to me and to anyone with whom I interact on any basis. I am willing to listen to anyone who wants to become the best version of themselves and help those people in whatever way I can.

Overall, I would feel good to know that I am able to impact and influence positive change in people's lives. I find happiness and a sense of satisfaction in being able to help others. As I became a woman of substance, my leadership qualities improved, I learned how to be available to my followers, and I was able to learn that as a leader, you have to be honest with your followers and not try to portray an image of perfection. We all are human and as such we are subject to err. I think some people respond to leaders more positively when they see that they are just as vulnerable as others and that they have also made mistakes. To my mind, such an approach to leadership lends itself to demonstrating to others that there is merit in making mistakes, as they present the opportunity for learning and growth to occur, showing how obstacles help to make you stronger.

I urge you not to settle, but to follow your dreams. How would you know what you are capable of achieving if you do not take a chance? As the author of "Business of the 21st Century" said, "Risk is equivalent to reward". The reality is that not everyone is ordained to be a pastor, prime minister, or president, but you can become a leader wherever you find yourself. Note that leadership is not a position or a title, it is action and setting an example. Being a leader is not specific to people who hold high positions; We often lead in some way daily, we simply did not recognise our actions as being those of a leader. Armed with this knowledge, I encourage you to make an even greater effort to become the leader you were created and/or can grow to be.

Chapter 26

Important People Met Along My Journey

On the journey of life, one thing I have learnt is that we need people to survive including family members, friends, mentors, your pastor, and any other influential persons that would impact our lives positively. This chapter seeks mainly to highlight some important people who are not family members, but who helped with my development along the way.

The first two persons I would like to mention are my two national managers Mrs. Vernetta Flanders and Jinelle James. Mrs. Flanders was not only my manager but I considered her to be like a mum to me. She has been a mentor to me and she was always there if I needed any advice and also guided me to make the best decisions. Over the years playing with the national team, Mrs. Flanders and I have built a really close relationship and she would be the first person I would approach if I needed advice or guidance in making an important decision. I would call her and we would chat sometimes for long hours. After talking to her, I always felt more confident with going ahead to make any decision. I appreciate the positive role she played in my life. I know I can call upon her at any time and am happy I have her in my life.

On the other hand, my next favorite manager/ mentor was Jinelle James. She was also a very influential person on my life's journey. I always consulted with her especially, when I wanted advice pertaining to business moves. Though our conversations were largely about business strategies, we could not have a conversation and not crack some jokes. Sometimes our conversations would turn into more humorous moments that proved to be for the soul as well. Jinelle is an educated woman who has many innovative ideas. She is another person whom I consider as my mentor. Both Mrs. Flanders and Jinelle played a really influential role in guiding me through life, and for that, I am truly appreciative.

Two other persons who have been important to me are Mr. Anthony Blake and Mr. Persad, both of whom have been instrumental to the success of my "Kick it With Karyn" tournament. Both Mr. Blake and Mr. Persad assisted me with finding sponsors and offered great advice on how to make the event more successful and better organized each year. During the six years that I have been doing the tournament, both Mr. Blake and Mr. Persad have guided me along the way. They have even been there to spearhead the preparations to ensure that there were no loopholes. I am grateful to Mr. Anthony Blake and Mr. Persad for the roles they have played in ensuring that each edition of my tournament has been successful.

It is important to note that no human knows everything and every human knows something. As a woman striving to add substance to her being and to her life, you ought not to ever feel that you are above seeking the assistance of people who may be more knowledgeable than you. Remember, a woman of substance is one who recognises her limitations and who is humble enough to seek help in the face of these, and therefore, her knowledge base expands. A woman of substance is also one who is not selfish with her knowledge, but who realises that in sharing what she knows, she enhances her own understanding, while actively contributing to creating a larger pool of women of substance who are equipped and prepared to overcome life's challenges.

Chapter 27

Meet April Heinrich

April Dawn Heinrich was one of the older heads in football. I have chosen to highlight her story simply because she became one of the legends in women's football in her era. As one successful both on and off the field, I thought to use her story not only to inspire others but to highlight her hard work and how her different successes did not come overnight. I must say that I was blessed to have been granted the opportunity to have a written interview with the all-time celebrity April Heinrich.

April grew up in Denver, Colorado, and started playing football at the age of five or six years old. April then played recreational soccer around the age of 13 and later played with Denver Bandits Academy. April attended Mesa College where she played college basketball, before opting to transfer after her first year, to play college soccer at North Carolina

– Chapel Hill. While playing college soccer, April won three college titles at the Division 1 National Championship in the years (1983,1984, & 1986). Years after she completed college, in 1998, she would go on to become the first woman to be inducted into the US Hall of Fame. When I asked April what it was like to achieve such a prestigious accolade, she stated it was a great honor and that being the first woman to receive this award, continues to feel special.

April was one of the first players to play on the United States soccer team, rising to the rank of team captain in 1986 and maintaining the title until 1991. The United States national team is ranked number one in the world so when asked what the selection process was like, competing against top names like Jill Ellis, Mere Ham, Cat Whitehill, and Shannon Box, April mentioned that it was always competitive vying for spots on the team, a challenge she welcomed. The trials were completed nationwide and roughly 50 to 100 players in a city would participate in a weekend-long trial. She said it was never easy securing a spot, but she ensured she put in the work so that she could consistently make the team because she understood that nothing comes easy, you have to work hard.

During our interview, I asked April what was one of her most memorable moments being on the US national team, to which she replied that it was being able to play and win a FIFA Women's World Cup. Many of us as footballers dream of making it to the world cup, but April dreamt it, made it, and also won the world cup, which is a really fantastic accomplishment. April opined that she wouldn't change the era in which she played, but expressed that she would like to play with some of the current United States players because she wanted to see if she would have the same footballing experience as when she was playing with players of her time.

From 1988 to 1989, April played professionally in Italy with two clubs, both Juventus Prato. This was huge because Juventus is one of the biggest and most recognised football clubs in the world, and to have been selected to play at that club is an awesome achievement. After she completed her professional career, she became a highly qualified coach becoming one of the first female coaches nationally. April credits her success to her belief that one should focus on the moment, train hard, play hard, compete with oneself, not others, embrace failures and lessons learned to make oneself better, be kind, be growth-oriented, ask questions, find a coach you can get positive feedback from regularly, and ask for feedback or input. April is now working with Concacaf to develop and implement programs.

April's story is proof that we are all purposed for greatness. She decided that she wanted to win at life and she was willing to do the work to be successful. In addition, April mentioned that she is a very competitive person, and she holds herself to high standards. One lesson April left with me was, "If you do not hold yourself to high standards, no one else will". I think this brings me back to the name of the book woman of substance. You have to be able to challenge yourself to push further than normal expectations especially if you have the desire and you are passionate about achieving particular life goals. Do not hold back yourself; to quote Nike's famous slogan "Just do it".

Another point made during our conversation which stood out to me was that April said she held herself accountable at all times. As humans many of us loathe accepting responsibility for the way our lives progress, preferring instead to play the blame game when things do not go our way. However, we have to hold ourselves accountable for all our actions and their ensuing consequences, whether good or bad. April continued to drop more nuggets, two of which stood out. She said "If you are doing something, you owe it to yourself to do it to the best of your ability." and "If you fail at something, don't quit, keep going!" These tidbits certainly resonated with me. April also stated that she prided herself on doing her best at all times. One of the most profound descriptions of herself which stood out to me was that "she embraces failures rather than fear failures". April showed that she was fearless and she never feared making mistakes, she would just go after what she wanted! I found such an attitude to be so contagious; how could one not want to emulate this fearless attitude. As one who strongly believes that young women ought to keep empowering themselves to lead to the achievement of their goals, April definitely walks her talk.

At the close of our conversation, April shared with me two quotes that form a significant part of her belief system and which she wanted to leave with me. The first was, "Even if you're on the right track, if you just sit there you will get run over". (Will Rogers). The second quote was "If you say you can't, it really means you won't. So, practice telling yourself you can!"

One of the main reasons I opted to include a chapter on April was to highlight who she was, how she became successful, how she is still achieving her goals, and what makes her a great example of a woman of substance. None of April's successes came overnight. She was fearless, relentless, and focused on using her passion and the avenue of football to help her to become successful, both on and off the field. We each must choose our own paths to become a woman of substance. April succeeded at what she was passionate about and we all need to find our passions and go after attaining our goals. April is another shining example of a woman who followed and fulfilled her dreams and was able to push herself to achieve goals beyond typical expectations.

My question is, are you willing to let yet another story of triumph go to waste, or are you willing to use this story to help shape, inspire and motivate you to find your passion?

During our conversation, April would have mentioned people whose life stories inspired her, and she used those as added motivation to help her keep pushing to achieve her own dreams. You may not want or be able to achieve all that April did, but you can do anything you want, fulfil your own purpose, once you put your mind to it. Challenge yourself to achieve that desired goal. Yes, start today! Don't wait! You can do it! The power of choice is in your hands, choose wisely!

Chapter 28

Caribbean Power House Creating History

You may be wondering who is this Caribbean "powerhouse" creating history. That would be the Jamaican women's national senior team that is creating history. When they became the first Caribbean country to qualify for the Women's World Cup in 2019 in France, it was a bitter-sweet moment because I had been hoping that Trinidad and Tobago would have had that honour. One of my dreams as a little girl had been to make it to the World Cup one day as part of the Trinidad and Tobago women's team. I loved playing against Jamaica because we had a bitter rivalry since both countries are the two top teams in the Caribbean. In spite of that, I applaud Jamaica for accomplishing this feat; all their hard work and effort paid off.

Having made this giant stride in women's football, the Jamaican female team has automatically created the opportunity for these ladies to not only enjoy the World Cup experience but to secure professional contracts, acquire endorsements, gain recognition, and in doing so earn more money to be able to help their families financially. The members of this team have also automatically ascended to becoming role models for others who are aspiring to accomplish similar and who may be facing comparable difficulties.

In order for the Jamaica women's football team to make it to the World Cup, they had to put in the work. The team faced a severe lack of resources which would have inevitably smoothened their road to success, but they didn't allow that deficiency to hinder their efforts. They are fantastic examples of women of substance who have had to wade through myriad difficulties in order to enjoy the success they sought. The Jamaican team reminds us that in our quest to become women of substance we must engage in war in order to enjoy the sweet taste of victory.

Chapter 29

Who is My Role Model?

If you had asked me this question years ago, my response would have differed from that of today. When I was younger, I would have just said someone who is a famous professional footballer. Now that I have grown and gained life experiences, I am now able to understand life a little better, and that automatically changes my answer about who is my role model. Over the years, I have developed a very strong, empowered, goal-oriented attitude, thus, I would now say that my role model is myself.

The circumstances I have existed under, the experiences I have had, and the obstacles I have overcome, have helped to build my character and my self-esteem, and I am a wiser individual today. I am more fearless, bold, courageous, self-motivated, and success-driven. Though there are leaders I admire, especially their life stories leading up to them becoming successful, and in spite of the fact that I often use those leaders I admire as a source of knowledge, I am very much aware of how far I have come in my development as an individual. Therefore, I take pride in being my own role model because I learnt to push myself beyond the limits that I once placed upon myself.

Through my life experiences, I have discredited the nickname "Baby", which many once knew me by because of the mere fact that I was seen as fragile, sensitive, and unable to cope with life's pressures. Now that I am setting goals, working tirelessly to accomplish my dreams, and achieving them, I think I am well placed to be considered a role model to others, so why not start with being my own role model.

Part of my accepting the challenge to be my own role model is so that I would always feel compelled to be and do my very best. I want to continue to keep pushing myself to achieve beyond that which I expect of myself. To my mind, I am the best person to hold me accountable because nobody has a better understanding of how important my goals are to me.

That is not to say that there aren't people whose lives I believe are worthy of emulation. There are quite a few people who have created their own legacies and whom I find very admirable. Football icon, Cali Lloyd, opined, "If you are not willing to learn no one can help you. If you are determined to learn, no one can stop you". I think this quote reflects my character perfectly since I am always open to acquiring knowledge. In my opinion, to keep learning is the only way to acquire modernized skills, to learn better people skills, and to generate novel ideas.

I however believe that a woman of substance is one who is intrinsically motivated, who does not require others to be the driving force behind her in order for her to do what she must to succeed. It is this mindset that would have been the driving force behind me starting the "Kick it With Karyn" tournament. I wanted to create my own legacy. There is a fire that burns in me that no man lit and which no man can fan. Being my own role model has made me hungry for success because my aim is not to follow others, but to make myself proud, and to pay homage to God for His generosity in blessing me with such amazing capabilities and talents.

Chapter 30

"Kick it With Karyn"

One day, I was on a flight deep in thought about what I could do to give back to my community and I thought, "why not do a football competition?" After all, football brings people together and presents the perfect opportunity for "lime" and "vibes". I thought the tournament would have been ideal to give back to the community I love so much. I could remember that the first years of hosting "Kick it With Karyn" were planned while I was away at college. That was not easy but I am good at delegating and I had a supportive team upon whom I could rely to get things organised until I was able to return home to do whatever was left to be done.

Having been in existence for a few years, the tournament has been the perfect setup, filling the void left by the lack of youth football and 7 a-side tournaments held in Tobago. The tournament which I cleverly renamed "Kick it With Karyn", has been a blessing, and each year I have been able to build on this event in numerous ways. For the first few years, the name of the tournament was "Forbes Soccer Picnic" but I felt that I needed to enhance the tournament by using a more attractive name. I consulted with a close cousin of mine, Shane Sandy, and we both came up with a few name suggestions. The name that stood out to me the most and which I thought would be the most marketable name was "Kick it With Karyn". To my mind, using my name at the end of the name of the tournament would have been great since as a national footballer, I am already well known. I also believe utilizing my name further helped, "Kick it With Karyn" by giving the tournament more recognition throughout Tobago and enabling me to receive sponsorship. Over the years the tournament has also helped me to continue to market my brand.

The tournament has been a community-building initiative, having a positive effect not just on the community of Plymouth, but on the wider community as well. Businesses such as hotels, car rental agencies, groceries, gas stations, stores, airlines, and the ferry service have all been able to generate funds by catering to the needs of those people who journey to Tobago annually to participate in or simply enjoy the tournament. Businesses that have signed on as sponsors have gained exposure through public display, media coverage, and other methods of advertisement.

I view the first tournament as a test case. It provided a guide to help make the other five tournaments more successful. Each year, thus far, the "Kick it With Karyn" tournament has grown tremendously, consistently growing bigger and better with each successive year. As I have become more experienced with hosting the tournament it has become more organized and more people are gaining a greater understanding of my drive and rationale behind creating this tournament. I do not only want my tournament to be locally recognized, but to be recognised throughout the Caribbean and globally someday. All that I am doing at present is preparing me for my future and establishing a foundation for potentially opening my own football league in years to come. I am beyond pleased that my tournament has been earning positive feedback, creating positive energy, and bringing the community together. It makes me quite happy to be able to contribute in that way. As time progresses and once blessed with good health and strength, I hope to be able to add more fun and inclusive activities to the schedule of events for the "Kick it With Karyn" tournament.

If you ask me, I would say that being able to formulate, orchestrate and manage my own tournament was never something that I envisioned I would have been doing. The first year, I planned that tournament in two months, but due to the magnitude to which the tournament has grown, I now have to plan six months in advance. I am really proud of myself for the hard work I have invested to make this tournament a success each year. However, I recognise that without God, my tournament would have not been successful; I give Him all the praise. The support from my friends, family, and community members is always overwhelming and I thank them for that.

The tournament has enabled me to interact with sponsors, connect with people in high society, bond with the public, learn time management skills and the importance of fundraising prior to hosting such events, and brainstorm new ideas and see them materialise. I would advise anyone that if you want to do anything, know that it starts with one step. That is what I did and I am thankful that I took that leap of faith and believed in myself. When I look back, this tournament has impacted my life positively in so many ways and I am thankful.

There is no success without struggle and challenges, but you ought not to let that stop you from pushing to achieve your goals. I had obstacles along my journey but they did not stop me from hosting my tournament. Be fearless! Do not let anything or anyone hold you back from fulfilling your dreams. One of my favorite quotes from Michael Jordan states, "I have failed over and over again and that's why I succeed". Everything does not always work out with one try, sometimes you have to keep at it, be dedicated, put in the work necessary to succeed, and everything would fall into place from there. On the road to success, there are speed bumps and they are all part of the process. You have to find solutions to your problems and keep it moving. You cannot stop challenges; you have no control over them. What you do have control over, is how you react to those challenges. Put in the work, have faith and everything would take its natural course.

Chapter 31

Future Plans

I Needed to Consult With Covid

Your plans may not turn out exactly how you envisioned them, but it is always good to have plans for the future and let those plans shape themselves. It is important to note that the journey of life never stops until you die. Even though I have achieved much as a "woman of substance" I am still dreaming and I have more goals that I would like to achieve. My current thoughts and actions are geared toward ensuring that I have a steady and adequate income that would enable me to take care of myself and help my mother. The more I develop into the person the Lord created me to be, the more I know that I am destined for greatness.

Having fulfilled one of my greatest dreams of playing football internationally in 2019, I was poised to leave again for Iceland in 2020 to fulfil my second already signed contract, when the month before I was scheduled to leave, the global pandemic, COVID-19, hit the world. In light of having my plans thwarted, I immediately started working on my next goal - the opening of my clothing store, "FFVC APPAREL". I took a leap of faith, sacrificed, and built my store. I was also able to utilize the downtime created by the pandemic to launch my clothing line, "DS" which means "doosumthng", with my business partner Marvin Small. Currently in 2021, after having high hopes of being able to rejoin my team, I am still at home and the store remains closed due to measures implemented by the government to curb further outbreaks of Covid-19. Though the store is closed at this time, I see now that it actually made sense to think about my future and focus on that goal in the meantime. We are still facing the effects of this pandemic so I am not sure how my career will go, but I know I have my clothing store which will help me generate an income.

Apart from having the store, I would like to become a motivational speaker so I could impact lives positively. I have so much to share and I aim to do this through further developmental programs, utilizing platforms on which I am able to lecture and recount my experience and journey to becoming a "woman of substance". There are many young lives out there that need to hear someone's story and I believe that that person may be me. Everyone has a story, but not everyone chooses to share his story. In any way possible, if I can, I want to help others find themselves, to really help them stay motivated towards their goals. In everything I do, I want to create a positive environment for those around me.

In the future, after playing professional football, I would also like to open a football academy geared towards girls. I have a plan already in motion to qualify myself by earning certificates in coaching. In doing so I would be able to stay up-to-date with the new and improved coaching tactics and developments. I am passionate about football but I also have a lot to offer by being a coach at the end of my playing career. Even though I may have these plans, I am not rushing, I would let the Lord lead me accordingly because my true aspiration is to create my own legacy, one of which I can be proud.

The avenue I am going to use to create my legacy is by motivating young people to find their passions. Lovingly shortened to "FYP" which stands for "Find Your Passion", is actually a slogan often used by Lauren Hutchinson while we played for the Trinidad and Tobago national senior football team together. I always felt inspired by her positive attitude and her drive to help others to find their passions. I must say, Lauren, the other girls on the team, and I, became sisters so I more or less knew all these girls inside out. Lauren and I were cool, we would often talk about business ideas and some of my future plans whenever we conversate. She is really a genuine and passionate person, especially about her own brand. One thing about her I must mention is the fact that she works really hard on and off the field. Lauren always encourages me in a big way to continue to build my tournament and take it to another level. Lauren currently has her own business and one of her initiatives in Richmond Virginia is helping young ladies to find their passion in football. She also hosts summer camps, prepares athletes, assists with finding top colleges for the athletes, takes her youth teams to tournaments, and more. I have interacted with her on a one-on-one basis, finding out the ways and means by which she developed such a huge following and learning about some of the steps she took to get her program to be successful.

As I develop my own tournament, I would be utilizing some of the knowledge I have garnered from Lauren to enhance 'Kick it With Karyn". With my interpretation of "find your passion", the concept can not only be used in sports but you can "find your passion" in anything you want to accomplish in life. For example, if a person wants to be a hairdresser, a farmer, or a carpenter, you name it, you can do it, you just have to find your passion. It doesn't matter what career path you choose, once you're passionate about it, go for it. Take the opportunity to capitalize on any chance you have to elevate yourself in any way. Nothing is wrong with taking chances and seeing where they lead you. Do not leave this earth regretting or feeling like you did not fulfill the dreams you had and achieve the goals you had set. It feels so good to know that you are doing something you love. So do not limit yourself, take that chance today and see where it leads you! This book is my start towards fulfilling my desire of wanting to inspire and motivate others. I think as women sometimes, we tend to settle for less, but I am here to say, I have grown into a "woman of substance" through every opportunity and experience I have been exposed to thus far. I am still very hungry to achieve more. I urge you to step out of your comfort zone, and take a leap of faith today!

Chapter 32

Plans for a Family

I am frequently asked the question if I would like to have a family. Of course, I would like to have a family. I would love to get married then have one child, though the second one would be negotiable between my husband and me. I feel the need to know the experience of having one child, then I would be able to explore the possibility of having a second one, but I'll cross that bridge when that time comes. I think one of the main reasons people ask if I want a family, is due to the fact that I am Thirty years old, single and still playing football, all factors I presume which don't augur well for building a family.

To be honest, after that one relationship mentioned earlier in this book, I did speak to a few other gentlemen, but those didn't work come to fruition because these men didn't possess the qualities I needed. I am single by choice, but I do want to be able to give someone who is worth my time, a chance. I have worked too hard on myself to allow any and everyone to enter into my life though. Not being in a relationship at present, is actually helping me to learn more about myself. Based on my experience, I am now very patient. I am not rushing because I believe that nothing happens before its time and I know that God's timing is perfect.

Yes, I want to be loved and to love someone the right way, because there are too many relationships that lack the real meaning of loving and caring about someone the right way. I am very old school; I believe in taking my time. In spite of my age, I am not worried. I want to be with someone with whom I am equally yoked and who deserves me. I refuse to jump into a relationship because my friends may be in one. I am a romantic, loving, caring, thoughtful person. I believe when a woman is loved the right way, she has a glow. Hence the reason women should not let their guard down and they need to hold themselves to a standard that men would have no choice but to respect them. Obviously, we cannot stop people from making their own decisions, but that also means that you too have control over your decisions. It is my firm belief that men tend to respect women, based on the way we present ourselves. You have to decide as a woman how you want to be addressed, by the manner in which you carry about yourself. I also think that your dress code can dictate the type of men you would like to attract.

Being a woman of substance, you must be able to stand firm and maintain your ideals, carry about yourself in a respectable manner, be ambitious as you endeavour to accomplish your goals, accept challenges and find solutions to problems that may arise. It is important to note that life doesn't always progress according to the plans we have set, but nothing is wrong with having a plan.

I am at the stage of my life where I am preparing myself to meet my husband. I am empowering myself to be a woman of substance who would also make a good wife. I have always been the faithful, "get settled down" type of woman. I am very family-oriented and I would endeavour to teach my children the right moral values. I would like the experience of having a family. I pray that the person who comes into my life would be someone who supports me and who would allow me to support him. I know that this may sound like a perfect little life, but I also know that once I place my desires in God's hands He will approve or disapprove as He sees fit.

Chapter 33

A Proud Moment - The Grand Finale

Without a doubt, one of the things that I am most proud of myself for having accomplished was being able to pen and publish this book, "Woman of Substance". I believe that we all have a story but I know that not everyone is willing to share his story; it's not always easy to put one's story into words. The mere fact that I mustered the courage and took the time to tell my story, is a proud moment for me. With no hint of cockiness, I believe that my story has the power to change lives. Even if it inspires one person, the book inspired SOMEONE, and that would be the fulfillment of one of my heart's greatest desires, to be able to inspire others. To know that someone read this book and can say, "Karyn is the reason why I did not give up" would be the greatest accolade I could receive.

The benefits of having written this book have been twofold, as in the process I both gave of myself as a woman of substance and became more of a woman of substance in the process. On my journey of becoming a woman of substance, I aspired to be a pillar of hope to anyone who may look up to me and to anyone who may be losing faith in the face of difficulties. There is so much that's wrong with the world that I want to leave a lasting positive impression on anyone with whom I come into contact.

In my Thirty years, I have had disappointments but, I believe that disappointments are a set up for an appointment somewhere else in life. I do not want to look back on my life and say that I should have done this or that; I want to take advantage of every good opportunity that presents itself and be able to use any lessons learnt to become a better person. My experiences thus far have caused me to develop a way of life called "emotional fitness". This simply means that I enjoy good moments and make the necessary mental adjustments when failures arise. All things, positive or negative, are preparing us for great things. Do not give up when things get rough, find solutions, and make sure you finish what you started. Trust the process, be open to what life has to offer, and above all, trust God.

After months of going to class and really applying myself, I sat the exams again, doing five subjects, and this time I succeeded at passing four out of the five subjects. Now in possession of six subjects, I decided to further my studies at the university level abroad and also to play football. However, I would first complete a year of Advanced level studies at 6th form until I was able to successfully complete my SATs and receive a scholarship. In 2012, I received my breakthrough to attend college abroad, and in January of that year, I left Tobago to attend Northwood University in Texas.

About The Author

Who is Karyn Forbes?

Hailing from the scenic seaside village of Plymouth, Tobago, I am twenty-nine-year-old Karyn Forbes, known by many as "Baby". While I consider myself to be mostly introverted, I acknowledge that I may possess some traits of an extrovert. I pride myself on being a very kind, authentic, loving, caring, genuine, and God-fearing person. I have a great personality, or so I have been told (lol.) Though I am by no means perfect, I do try to live right, as guided by my spiritual values and I always try to maintain a positive attitude. Over the years, my knowledge base in various aspects of my life has deepened and strengthened, and in the chapters of this book, you would have the opportunity to not only read more of my story but to gain some insight into the knowledge I have garnered. Indeed, I have come a long way and I am grateful for the growth that I have experienced.

I am not a lover of crowds, therefore, I am not a partygoer. I am a sports person, I love sports. I ran track and field, but I knew it wasn't what I wanted to do, so I never pursued it further than high school. I also played cricket. I was good at it but I did not like it as much as football. Football is my first love sport. Perhaps it is the fact that I grew up in a family of footballers that first fuelled my interest in and passion for the sport. What I'm quite certain of, is that when I play football, it makes me happy.

Apart from playing football, I am also passionate about business, and having completed a degree in Business Management, I am now the proud owner of my own clothing line and a recently opened store, as well as being the mastermind behind an annual football tournament cleverly named after me.

In my leisure time, I enjoy socializing by going to the beach, visiting the mall, watching football, hanging out with friends, going to church, travelling, and watching movies. I am a very simple person and I enjoy living a simple life. To my mind, simplicity is always effective and I have found that it works well for me.

Often, because of my laid-back personality, I can seem shy or very reserved, until I assess the situation, and then I would act accordingly. I can be firm at times but even then I remain a very approachable person. I wasn't always a strong person but having had to live through adversities, I have developed myself into a resilient person. Previously I demonstrated reluctance to "come out of my shell", but my self-development over time has enabled me to overcome my fears, and I have emerged outspoken, confident, goal-oriented, independent, success-driven, focused, and stronger over time.

I applaud myself for my personal development over the years and for all of my achievements thus far. I credit my improvement to my having done one major thing - I let God be my guide. I surrendered completely to His will and coupled this with making a concerted effort to believe in myself.

www.ingramcontent.com/pod-product-compliance
Ingram Content Group UK Ltd.
Pitfield, Milton Keynes, MK11 3LW, UK
UKHW041945230426
12048UKWH00008B/144